THE JUNIOR BIRDER'S HANDBOOK

A Kid's Guide to Birdwatching

DANIELLE BELLENY

Illustrations by **MICHELLE CARLOS**

RP | KIDS
PHILADELPHIA

This book is dedicated to my nieces and nephews.
—D.B.

Running Press Kids
Hachette Book Group
1290 Avenue of the Americas, New York, NY 10104
www.runningpress.com/rpkids
@runningpresskids

Printed in China

First Edition: November 2023

Published by Running Press Kids, an imprint of Perseus Books, LLC,
a subsidiary of Hachette Book Group, Inc. The Running Press Kids name and logo
are trademarks of the Hachette Book Group.

The Hachette Speakers Bureau provides a wide range of authors for
speaking events. To find out more, go to www.hachettespeakersbureau.com or
email HachetteSpeakers@hbgusa.com.

Running Press books may be purchased in bulk for business, educational, or
promotional use. For more information, please contact your local bookseller or
the Hachette Book Group Special Markets Department at Special.Markets@hbgusa.com.

The publisher is not responsible for websites (or their content)
that are not owned by the publisher.

Print book cover and interior design by Frances J. Soo Ping Chow.

Library of Congress Control Number: 2023931583

ISBNs: 978-0-7624-8078-4 (hardcover), 978-0-7624-8079-1 (ebook)

1010

10 9 8 7 6 5 4 3 2 1

CONTENTS

INTRODUCTION

Birds are some of the most amazing creatures on this planet. One remarkable thing about birds is that you can find them almost anywhere. They live on every continent, including Antarctica! They thrive in busy cities, in remote country towns, in sprawling countryside, over the vast ocean, and everywhere in between.

Can you think of the last time you went a whole day without seeing or hearing a bird? It might be tough to imagine. This is because we are always surrounded by nature—even at times when it doesn't seem like it. When you move a little slower and look a little closer, you will begin to notice nature even in ordinary places. Sometimes we just need help knowing what to keep an eye out for. Learning more about the natural world around you can become an exciting hobby. *Bird-watching* or *birding* is the act of looking at and listening to birds for your own enjoyment. You may even be a budding *ornithologist*—that's a person who studies birds—without realizing it.

Do you know how to recognize the birds in your hometown? Do you know what to do when you find an injured bird? Do you know the differences between ravens and crows? No matter what your level of experience or interest, this book will help you identify birds in a variety of habitats and seasons. You'll learn the different behaviors of

birds—from why smaller birds chase hawks to extreme ways that birds survive cold weather—as well as migration trends and their impact on local ecosystems.

The first section of this book teaches how to identify North American birds. Since there are more than two thousand different kinds of birds on this continent, the focus will be on some of the more common species you can find. You will become familiar with what birds to expect whether you are exploring a forest, farm, beach, or town.

The second section of this book highlights eight unique ecosystems in North America and has detailed accounts of some specific birds that call each region home. Each ecosystem is like a tiny planet with unique plants and weather that shape them. The birds that rely on those ecosystems have special traits that make them exceptionally fit for where they live.

With the activities in this book, you'll be able to make your neighborhood more welcoming to birds. Create your own window decals that show your artistic flair but also stop birds from running into the glass. Build a bird feeder from recycled materials that are probably in your home right now. You can also read about bird-friendly plants that would be great additions to the green spaces you love. If you want to learn a great way to study the nature closest to you, check out the nature journal activity. You can personalize your own journal, write entries about your experiences with nature, and draw your favorite plants and animals.

PART I

The Basics

Where and How to Go Birding

· · • • • ·

You can enjoy birds anytime and anywhere! You can go birding in everyday places like your favorite park, the grocery store parking lot, at your bedroom window, and even virtually through live webcams. You can do it with or without equipment. Since birds are always around, you'll likely find something to observe wherever you are. One of the most important things to remember as a birder, however, is to respect the environment.

You can build a stronger connection to the land by acknowledging the life it supports and by being mindful about the ways you interact with it. When you have found a birding spot, take a moment to be still and thank the land around you for sustaining life. Being in nature makes people feel refreshed, and birding can be a form of meditation to improve your mood and mind. There are even scientific studies that show there are mental and physical benefits to being outside.

REMINDER: While you're out and about, be sure to not leave any trash behind, give the animals you notice plenty of space, and refrain from luring them closer to you.

How to Identify Birds

· · • • • ·

There are over 10,000 species of birds in the world! While it may be nearly impossible to remember every different kind, learning the birds that live near you can be a very fun hobby. You just have to know where to start! As with everything else you learn, your birding skills will get better with practice. You can begin by studying one or two of the birds around your neighborhood. Once you feel confident in your ability to recognize them, you can turn your focus to other birds in the area.

The only tool needed to be a successful birder is a curious mind. That said, there are a few additional items that can be useful to get you started. First, grab some writing supplies—a journal or notebook or some loose pieces of paper, as well as a pencil, pen, markers, or whatever you have handy—to take notes and/or sketch. Second, find a bird field guide that has pictures and information about birds of the region where you live. A great place to start is at your local library, but you can also find field guides online or at bookstores. Third, get a pair of binoculars. Binoculars are handheld telescopes that give us a closer look at distant objects. Birding binoculars magnify what you can see to reveal details that people would not notice with their naked eye. That's it. That's all you need!

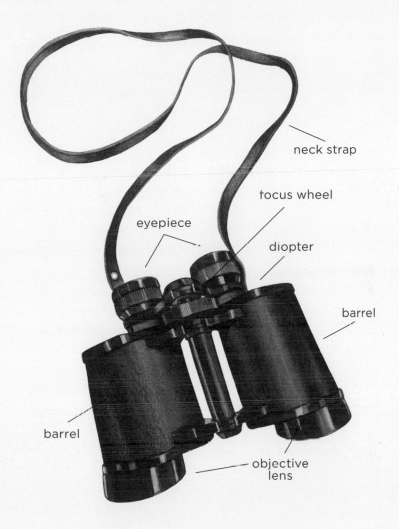

neck strap

focus wheel

eyepiece

diopter

barrel

barrel

objective lens

CHOOSING (AND USING) BINOCULARS

There are two numbers on binoculars—the first number represents magnification of the eyepiece, and the second number represents the size of the objective lens. Now, you may think that binoculars with high magnifications would be better for bird-watching, but that is not the case because these binoculars weigh more and are

HOW TO USE BINOCULARS

• • • • • •

Start by holding the binoculars to your eyes and keeping both eyes open as you adjust the two eyepieces so that they line up with your eyes. You will know that the eyepieces are perfectly in place when the black edges in your view are gone on both sides. After this adjustment is done, you should see a perfect circle image of the objects in your field of vision. If your binoculars are still too big for your face or you have trouble looking through both barrels, try turning the two binoculars on their side and using just one eye to look through the top barrel.

Now find something in the distance to practice focusing on. Use something large and still like a tree, building, stop sign, light pole, or parked car. Spin the main focus wheel to either side and notice how your view changes. The center focus wheel helps to focus both the left and right eyepieces at the same time. In general, spinning the wheel to the left moves the focus to objects farther away and spinning the wheel to the right moves the focus closer.

Some binoculars have a small adjustable wheel near the right eyepiece. This is the diopter adjustment, and it helps finely focus the image in your binoculars. To adjust the diopter, start by looking through the left eyepiece while your right eye is closed. Use the main focus wheel to get an image in focus. Next, close your left eye and open your right eye as you spin the diopter wheel left or right until the image is in focus again. Lastly, open both eyes, and if the image is not crystal clear, then you will need to repeat the process. If it is perfectly in focus, then congratulations! You're one step closer to mastering binoculars!

more difficult to keep steady. It's best to use a pair of binoculars that you can hold comfortably for a while. Young birders are recommended to use binoculars with two to eight times magnification.

The size of the objective lens decides how much light enters the binoculars. Images in your binoculars will appear brighter and more vibrant as the objective lens size increases. Birding binoculars usually have objective lenses from 21 and 42 millimeters. Try binoculars with objective lens sizes between 21 to 32 mm.

Finding birds with binoculars can be tricky, but you'll get the hang of it with practice.

THE GISS METHOD

Now, some people may think the markings on a bird's feathers would be enough to identify the species. But looking at feathers alone won't solve the mystery, especially for bird species that look very alike. Instead, birders rely on the GISS method to positively ID birds. GISS stands for *general impression of size and shape.* Focusing on specific details and behaviors of the bird helps narrow down the list of potential species. You have likely used this method without even realizing. For example, if you see a group of large, dark birds circling in the sky above some roadkill, you would likely assume those birds are a kind of vulture. You may not know which species of vulture, but you already know they are not woodpeckers, sparrows, or chickens. The GISS method will not always tell you the exact type of bird you are looking at, but it will help you get closer to identifying the bird in front of you. Once you get the hang of this method, you'll be on your way to becoming a birding pro.

Let's practice the GISS method. Find a window, place outside, or bird webcam where you can sit and watch birds for five minutes.

TIP: Try looking for online bird webcams hosted by a local nature center. A list of places to watch bird webcams can be found in the back of the book.

Try to draw or write down the following things for one or two different birds you notice:

- **LOCATION.** Where is the bird? Is it in a tree, on the ground, or flying?
- **ACTIVITY.** What is the bird doing? Is the bird sitting on a wire, climbing a tree, swimming across a pond, or eating at a bird feeder?
- **SIZE.** Is the bird very tiny, small, medium, large, or very large? Can you compare the bird's size to something in your home?
- **SHAPE.** Describe or sketch the shape of the bird's body, legs, head, and bill. You don't have to draw it perfectly! The hope is you'll be able to compare your observations to the field guide.
- **COLOR.** What are the main colors you notice? For multicolored birds, try to write down where each color is. You can also color in the sketch of the bird with markers, colored pencils, or crayons.

- **TAIL SHAPE.** The tail can be difficult to see sometimes, but they come in an assortment of shapes including squared, rounded, forked, and tapered. Draw or write what shape you notice.
- **FLIGHT PATTERN.** Describe how often the bird beats its wings or glides when flying. You can also draw the patterns of its flight. For example, vultures fly in a spiral shape.

Take your completed sketch and notes and try to match it with birds in your field guide. Start by looking for birds that have a similar shape and size to your notes. Once you have found a group of birds with the same general shape, begin paying closer attention to their color. When you notice a bird with similar colors, look for information about where the bird is found and how they usually behave. If the bird in the guide closely matches the appearance and behavior of the bird in your journal, then congratulations! You identified a bird!

Habitats:
Where Birds Belong

••●••

Every living thing requires food, water, shelter, and space in which to live. Almost every place on Earth—from desert to ocean—is home to some creature. The place where an organism gets all the things needed to survive is called its *habitat*. Some living things can only survive in very specific habitats— where the air is a certain temperature, the soil a particular type, or a certain food can be found. These plants and animals are very vulnerable to changes in their environment. In comparison, there are other living things that can survive in a wide variety of habitats.

Depending on the species, birds can be very picky about the places they like to nest, eat, breed, and migrate. Birds that have specific living requirements are called *specialists*. Specialist birds, like Rufous Hummingbirds (page 95), often have uncommonly shaped body parts or interesting behaviors that help them perfectly fit into their unique lifestyle. In comparison, birds that can easily live in many different kinds of environments, like Mourning Doves (page 81), are *generalists*. Generalist birds have plain-looking body parts and less complicated needs to help them get through whatever life throws their way.

The unusual looks and lifestyles of specialist birds like the Rufous Hummingbird didn't happen by accident. Instead, their

unique traits were developed slowly over time as each generation of specialist birds adapted more and more to their environment. With their strange adaptations, specialist birds found ways to thrive in their habitats.

Having different abilities can be really helpful, as it can mean having access to resources other animals can't get to. On the flip side, however, having unique abilities can also limit where and how specialist birds live. For example, hummingbirds have long and pointed bills to help them sip nectar from flowers. Not many other animals have that talent! But since their main food comes from flowers, hummingbirds would not be able to thrive in certain environments without such flowers—like a grassy farm pasture that would be perfect for birds that like to eat seeds, bugs, and plants. Generalist birds would find food all over the pasture. In a way, generalist birds have their own special ability—being able to find food, water, shelter, and space nearly anywhere.

Animals do not understand what a city, country, or continent are. These are ideas that humans created to refer to certain places. To view the world with the eyes of birds, we have to look at the unique natural features of the land. *Biomes* are "maps" or sections of land created by nature that are defined by the types of ecosystems they support. In North America, there are at least eight different biomes: Tundra, Boreal Forest, North Pacific Coast, American West, Mexican Drylands, Great Plains, Southeast Savannas & Forests, and Northeast American Forest. We can think of these regions as "life zones." The species living in these zones have a close relationship to one another.

Some animals and plants are restricted to certain biomes, while others can live in multiple biomes. *Migratory birds* are birds that travel to find the best resources for the season. They can go thousands of miles to reach their destination. Most wild birds found in North America are migratory. They will often live in two or more biomes because that is where they find the best foods and environmental conditions to support their lives. Birds will move from place to place based on the availability of water, insects, seeds, mates, and shelter. These are examples of resources that are the bare necessities for bird life. Other birds, especially *nonmigratory birds,* are restricted to a single biome. These birds are specialized to the area and have unique adaptations that make them perfectly suited to thrive in one biome.

TUNDRA

The Tundra biome expands across northern Canada and northern Alaska. This region is mountainous, treeless, and icy. The northernmost sections are almost entirely absent of plant and animal life—sometimes called *flora and fauna.* The landscape contains a combination of deep valleys, tall glaciers, vast grasslands, and numerous wetlands. The summers are short, having up to 85 days with 24 hours of continuous sunlight. The abundance of sunlight brings a sudden greening of the landscape. Typical summer temperatures are below 60 degrees Fahrenheit (15.6°C). The winters are long and dark, having up to 87 days where the sun never rises. Average winter temperatures are below freezing. Snow may fall any month of the year and stays on the ground for over eight months. In some places, the ground is permanently frozen (also known as *permafrost*). The tundra region is especially important for ducks, geese, and seabirds since the area supports large colonies containing millions of nesting birds. Birds specialized to live in the tundra will have dense feathers. Typical mammals in this region include polar bears, caribou, arctic hares, lemmings, and arctic foxes.

BOREAL FOREST

The Boreal Forest biome spans from the western coast of Alaska to the eastern coast of Canada. Boreal forests are the Earth's northernmost forest and are mostly made of slender, pine cone–like trees that are well adapted to the cold. The dense forests support mammals including black bears, moose, marten, chipmunks, lynx, and bobcats. Aside from densely wooded areas, this region also contains marshes, lakes, bogs, and rivers throughout. Boreal forests are especially important because they purify a lot of water and air. The numerous lakes and wetlands also attract hundreds of thousands of ducks, geese, swans, and loons. The birds come to nest and feed near the frigid waters. Winters in this area are long and cold with average temperatures below freezing for the whole season. Summers are short and cool.

NORTH PACIFIC COAST

The North Pacific Coast biome spans from southwestern Canada, along the west coast of the United States, and ends in the Baja Peninsula of Mexico. Mountains dominate the region, which then transitions to forests, valleys, and grassy plains in lower elevations. This region contains all the temperate rain forests in North America. On average, the rain forest will get over 100 inches (254 cm) of rain each year. The forested areas make up the majority of this region with pines, firs, and cedars as the most common trees. This region is especially important because it supports a variety of ancient plants and animals. The towering redwood trees growing here can be over 1,000 years old, and many other kinds of trees here can be several hundreds of years old. Winters and summers are mild. Typical mammals of the area include grizzly bears, elks, black-tailed deer, and wolves. Seabirds like puffins and gulls are very common.

AMERICAN WEST

The American West biome spans from western Canada to the southwestern United States. This region spans the Rocky Mountains and a unique mix of forests, sand dunes, grasslands, mountains, and desert shrublands. However, low shrubs and grasses are the dominant vegetation type. Many of the historic grasslands in the north no longer exist because the land has been converted to agriculture. This region is home to the Sagebrush Steppe, a fragile ecosystem for many unique and endangered plants and animals. Water has slowly carved rocks into canyons and cliffs. The Grand Canyon, a famous national monument, is a prime example of how water shapes stones over time. Winters in this region are cold and long. Summers are mild but short. Common mammals include pronghorn antelopes, mule deer, badgers, and coyotes.

MEXICAN DRYLANDS

The Mexican Drylands biome spans across the southwestern United States through northern Mexico. This region contains the scorching hot deserts of Southern California, like the Sonoran and Mojave Deserts, and the scrubby forest in the Sierra Madre Occidental mountain range. Plants and animals that live here must be adapted to long periods without rain. Dozens of cactus species are special to this region. This region can experience below freezing weather in the winters and very hot summers. Common mammals include jackrabbits, ground squirrels, coyotes, and mule deer.

GREAT PLAINS

The Great Plains biome spans from south-central Canada to the central United States. Overall, the plains remain fairly flat. Strong gusts of wind, drought, bison migrations, frosts, and wildfires shaped the plant and animal life for the region. The northern part of this region is now farmland but used to have tall aspen and oak trees mixed with open grasslands. The winters in the northern part are long and cold with almost constant snow. The summers are warm but short. The southern part is all prairies and grasslands with some oaky woodlands mixed in between. The summers in the south are pretty hot but the winters are milder. Grassland birds rely on the prairies in this region to build nests. Common mammals include pronghorn antelopes, prairie dogs, ground squirrels, and coyotes.

SOUTHEAST SAVANNAS & FORESTS

The Southeast Savannas & Forests biome is found in states along the Gulf of Mexico, along the Atlantic Ocean, and inland north to

Missouri. The region is very humid and has hot, tropical summers and mild winters. It is dominated by pine, oak, and elm forests. Hardwood swamp forests form along the many rivers in the area. Historically, the longleaf pine grasslands dominated the southeastern coasts. Common mammals include porcupines, chipmunks, white-tailed deer, and raccoons. Two essentials for wildlife—food and shelter—are relatively abundant in the Eastern Temperate Forests. Because it is a significant evolutionary area for the continent's fauna, the region contains a great diversity of species within several groups of animals. Mammals of the region include white-footed mice, gray squirrels, eastern chipmunks, raccoons, porcupines, gray foxes, bobcats, white-tailed deer, and black bears.

NORTHEAST AMERICAN FOREST

The Northeast American Forest biome is found from southeastern Canada to the south-central United States. This region has warm summers and mild to snowy winters. There are multiple types of forests that dominate the area. Historically, the American chestnut dominated the forests of the Appalachian Mountains. Unfortunately, a tree disease virtually wiped out most American chestnuts by the 1950s. Pine, birch, hickory, oak, and maple trees now dominate the remaining forests. The numerous wooded areas provide wildlife many natural sources of food and shelter. Common mammals include black bears, white-tailed deer, moose, gray foxes, and gray squirrels.

Protecting Birds

• • • • • •

I t's an unfortunate fact that bird populations around the world are rapidly vanishing. Worldwide, around 48 percent of bird species are declining. In North America, 30 percent of birds have disappeared in the last 50 years. Species that were very abundant have experienced dramatic population losses and will continue to dwindle without conservation efforts. Habitat loss and climate change are two major factors.

Habitat loss happens when humans expand cities or clear the land for farming, taking away wild spaces birds have relied on and creating new hazards for them. Cutting down trees, filling in wetlands, damming rivers, planting crops, and mowing fields are examples of activities that disrupt natural ecosystems. The disruption can introduce new obstacles like speeding cars, tall buildings, new predators, and pollution to the ecosystem. When habitat loss happens, birds lose safe places to breed, eat, roost, and migrate. Climate change refers to the alteration in the usual weather conditions of a region including rainfall and temperature.

Habitat loss and climate change damage more than just bird populations. Degraded habitats negatively impact drinking water and air quality, weaken soil health, and introduce predators and diseases to ecosystems. This may all sound like bad news, but there is hope—reversing the decline of bird populations is possible! We can take action in small but beneficial ways to save birds by adjusting how we live day-to-day and encouraging our communities to live in harmony with nature.

Windows on buildings are a major cause of bird deaths. Up to one billion birds are killed each year by crashing into the windows of homes and skyscrapers. While windows give us nice views of the outside world, they can be very confusing for birds because they reflect images of the sky, trees, and grass both day and night. Birds think the reflection is more space to fly through when it is actually a hard surface they fly into. Even if a bird is fortunate enough to not die on impact, they could be silently suffering from internal injuries and die shortly after. Thankfully, there are many ways to prevent window collisions!

Here are two ways to make your windows bird-safe:

• Turn off all unnecessary indoor and outdoor lights at night. This reduces the reflection and helps birds see the stars they use during migration.

• Apply window decals to your windows. There are special decals that are highly visible to birds but nearly invisible to humans and can be bought in stores. Better yet, use the activity on page (119) to make your own.

Predators are another major threat to birds. Hundreds of thousands of birds are picked off by predators during migration. Some predators are doing what they're designed to do—eat birds. Birds have evolved alongside native predators like snakes, coyotes, and raccoons. In healthy ecosystems, a balance between predators and prey is naturally maintained. However, one kind of predator is far more lethal than the rest: nonnative predators are a leading cause of bird deaths. And this group can include animals that we commonly have as pets. Pet cats are well-known predators of birds and other wildlife. If you have a cat that roams freely outside, it has probably left you an uneaten dead animal as a "gift." Allowing pets to go unsupervised outdoors is harmful to the environment. It is estimated that over one billion birds are killed by cats every year. If you would like for your kitty to get some outdoor time, be sure to supervise the cat and never let them out of your sight. You can even train your cat to wear a leash!

INJURED AND ABANDONED BIRDS

If you happen to find an injured or abandoned bird, get the help of a professional wildlife rehabilitator or veterinarian. They should be able to best advise you on next steps. Usually, the best thing to do is leave the bird where it is. Often, humans will think a bird is injured or abandoned when it is actually fine. In other situations, the bird may need the help of a licensed professional.

Signs that a bird may be injured or sick:
- Resting on the ground and does not fly away when approached
- Eyes are closed, squinted, swollen, or crusty
- Tries to fly but can't
- Feathers are very fluffed up
- Signs of blood, wounds, or injured limbs (hanging wing, dangling leg)

If the professional advises that the animal should be moved, be sure to get help from an adult and always wear gloves. Injured birds may scratch, bite, or peck at humans even when we are trying to help. This is the animal's way of defending itself from something they think is dangerous. In most situations, the best thing you can provide an injured bird is a warm, dark, and quiet place to rest. Move the bird to the bottom of a leafy bush where it can hide from predators and stay out of direct sunlight. If a bird needs to be taken to a care facility, place them in a cardboard box and drape a towel on top of the box. There's usually no need to provide the bird with food or water unless you are told to do so by a wildlife rehabilitator or veterinarian. Giving a bird food or water could actually make it sicker! Especially avoid offering wild birds bread, raw meat, and most other human foods whether they're healthy or sick.

Every year, especially during the spring and summer, many young birds are accidentally "bird-napped" by well-meaning people trying to help. Baby birds are always best cared for by their parents. But birds care for their young in ways that can look neglectful in the eyes of humans.

Hatchlings and *nestlings* are very young birds that are practically helpless without their parents. They have very few feathers and are unable to stand or walk. If you notice a hatchling or nestling has fallen from its nest, contact a professional wildlife rehabilitator for what to do next. Sometimes, baby birds are purposefully removed from the nest by their parents or siblings. While that may seem harsh, the parents and siblings are able to sense when a baby bird is sick or weak and will remove that bird from the nest. The remaining babies in the nest can then stay healthy and grow up stronger. Caring for wildlife is not the same as taking care of a domestic pet. Never try to raise any wild animals yourself.

Fledglings are young birds that are almost ready to leave the nest. They have grown most of their feathers, are able to hop around, can perch on trees, and are able to glide and flutter with their new wings. It is common for fledglings to leave their nests before they're able to fly well. The fledgling may appear to be sitting on the ground alone for long periods of time, but they usually have a parent nearby watching over them. So, if you find a young bird that matches the description of a fledgling, you can just let it be. This is a normal stage for birds and one of the last stages before they fly out into the world on their own!

HELPING BIRDS NEAR YOU

Another way to support birds is by growing native plants that thrive naturally in your region. These plants have evolved over hundreds or thousands of years to live in unison with the native wildlife of the area and provide sustainable food and shelter to animals. In return, the animals disperse the plant seeds. This balance keeps ecosystems healthy and intact. Nonnative plants can disrupt the relationships between wildlife and native plants. Ecosystems that are dominated by nonnative plants can become unbalanced and cause the native plants and animals to eventually become extinct.

Native plants are, essentially, natural bird feeders. When gardens and yards include native plants, birds are provided with natural habitats with year-round resources. However, many gardens and yards are full of nonnative plants. Removing nonnative plants and replacing them with native plants doesn't just help birds but also helps the planet by keeping the soil healthy, removing excess carbon dioxide from the air, and using less water. (Nonnative plants may require more water to survive outside their natural area.) Adding just one native plant to a landscape will greatly benefit the wildlife in your region. Imagine how planting a diverse collection of native plants in a garden can positively impact your community.

Native Plants for Your Birder Garden

•••••

Here are examples of regional, native plants to consider planting in your birder garden. Before planting, check to see what options are most compatible to your area.

AREAS	FLOWERS	SHRUBS AND TREES
Northeast Woodlands and Forests	Bloodroot, Canada mayflower, eastern red columbine, eastern shooting star, jack-in-the-pulpit, mayapple, spotted geranium, wild strawberry, and wintergreen	Black huckleberry, bush honeysuckle, hay-scented fern, maple trees, redbud, red elderberry, spicebush, sweet pepperbush, white oak, and witch hazel
North Pacific Coast	Beach strawberry, bunchberry, fireweed, inside-out flower, pearly everlasting, western bleeding heart, western trillium, wood sorrel, and yarrow	Nootka rose, osoberry, red huckleberry, red-twig dogwood, salmonberry, serviceberry, sword fern, and vine maple
American West	Heart-leaf bittercress, pink mountain-heather, purple monkeyflower, Rocky Mountain columbine, sanddune wallflower, shrubby cinquefoil, silky lupine, splitleaf Indian paintbrush, wild blue flax, and willow herb	American persimmon, American plum, black hawthorn, chokecherry, green ash, serviceberry, and soaptree yucca
Mexican Drylands	Basketflower, blackfoot daisy, chocolate daisy, great blanket flower, purple poppy mallow, purple prairie clover, slender dayflower, and yellow beeplant	Arroyo willow, black cherry, blue palo verde, catclaw acacia, desert willow, hoptree, sugar sumac, and velvet mesquite
Great Plains	American groundnut, anise hyssop, field pussytoes, heath aster, partridge pea, purple milkweed, white snakeroot, white sage, and trumpet vine	American hazelnut, big sagebrush, bur oak, gray dogwood, lady fern, New Jersey tea, and Ohio buckeye

Migration

••●••

As the seasons change, birds get the natural urge to move to a new home. This move is commonly known as *migration*. Bird migrations are spectacular events when birds leave one area to find another place with more resources. The feathered travelers are mainly in search of better food and, depending on the season, possibly a mate.

Insects and berries are the main foods for most birds but are much less abundant in North America during the winter. To survive, birds will fly south to warmer climates in the areas near the equator or to South America where the seasons are the reverse of those in North America. In these warmer spots, insects and berries are plentiful. Birds that hang out in Ontario during spring can fly all the way to Ecuador when the Canadian province begins to cool off. After the coldest months have ended, migratory birds will fly north again at the beginning of spring. Springtime in North America brings tons of new life. Trees grow new leaves, flowers begin to bloom, and bugs become more active. The surplus of food and shelter provides migratory birds the perfect environment to find mates, make nests, and raise chicks.

Migrations are miraculous events because of the extreme distances birds can travel. Tiny birds that are smaller than your fist are pushed to their limits to complete the annual journey. Before leaving for their "other" home, birds need to bulk up to make sure they have the energy to complete the trip. A few weeks before migrating, birds will eat enough to double their weight. The extra fat they gain is stored under their skin and gives them energy to fly across cities, mountain ranges, and oceans to reach their destinations.

Many birds will travel along ancient sky highways to journey from their spring breeding grounds to their wintering grounds. Most birds do not complete their migration in one continuous effort. Instead, they will find stops along their route to rest, refuel, and avoid bad weather. These pathways are called migratory *flyways*. Birds have a number of different standard routes they follow in the Western Hemisphere: the Pacific Flyway, Central Flyway, Mississippi Flyway, and Atlantic Flyway. A rest stop could be anywhere! Birds could even choose your neighborhood as a place to temporarily stop.

With so much distance to cover, you may wonder how in the world birds know where to go. During the day, birds can use the position of the sun to navigate by. During the night, birds use stars and constellations to know which direction to go. If you were a bird, where would you migrate?

QUIZ

MIGRATION DESTINATION VACATION

Answer the following questions to let your birder personality
determine the best location for your next vacation!

1. When is the best time of year for a vacation?

A. Fall

B. Spring

C. Summer

D. Winter

2. Where would you want to visit?

A. The forest to hike some trails

B. The countryside to get away from the city noise

C. The beach to swim in the cool water

D. The mountains to go skiing

3. How do you prefer to travel?

A. Road-tripping in an RV

B. Flying in an airplane

C. Taking the train

D. Riding in a boat

4. What kind of snacks do you like?

A. Granola bars

B. Potato chips

C. Fruit snacks

D. Veggie sticks

5. What color combination best represents you?

A. Red and orange

B. Green and yellow

C. Pink and white

D. Blue and purple

ANSWERS

MOSTLY As: Northeast American Forest—This region has many forests full of towering trees. In the fall, the leaves will begin to change color from green to gold, red, and orange. There are also well-traveled hiking trails through the many woods and mountains in this region. The Appalachian Trail—the longest hiking-only trail in the world—is located in this region. Hikers need plenty of nutritious snacks, like granola, to hike all 2,194 miles (3,531 km).

MOSTLY Bs: Great Plains—The plains are flat and support many food-producing farms. Aside from farmland, the Great Plains encompass open grasslands and prairies. Springtime in the prairies is a vibrant and colorful experience. The landscape is brought to life with green foliage and multihued blooms.

MOSTLY Cs: Mexican Drylands—The drylands are exactly what they sound like! Despite the lack of moisture and extreme heat, life thrives in this region. The drylands are an interesting combination of pine-oak forests, scrublands, deserts, and mountain ranges. This region also supports many farms that produce a variety of fruit and vegetables.

MOSTLY Ds: Tundra—The landscape covers a combination of deep valleys, tall glaciers, vast grasslands, and numerous wetlands. In this icy wonderland, snow may fall any month of the year. The flora and fauna in this region have special adaptations to survive the winters.

PART II

Selected Birds

American Dipper

. . ▪ ▪ ▪ .

PRONUNCIATION: *dip-ur*
RANGE: From Alaska to California and
southward to central Mexico
HABITAT: Streams, waterfalls, rivers,
ponds, and ocean banks
FOOD: Streambed insects, mosquitoes,
minnows, fish eggs
VOICE: A varied mix of trills and repeated notes

American Dippers are small gray birds with brownish-gray heads.
They have round bodies, thin black bills, long legs, and short squared
tails. American Dippers have white feathers on their eyelids! When
they blink, it looks like they are wearing fancy white makeup.

Their appearance is simple, but their lifestyle is unusual. At first glance, American Dippers look like any typical bird that hops on the ground, but the truth is that American Dippers have extraordinary habits and are unlike any other North American songbird. They are the only songbirds that have fully aquatic habits with lives revolving entirely around fast-moving, unpolluted streams and waterfalls.

American Dippers are sometimes called Water Thrushes because of how they dive, swim, and walk when they go underwater. While underwater, American Dippers search for insects, fish eggs, and minnows to eat. Between dives, they can be seen bobbing their tails and wings almost constantly as they walk on rocks and logs. The drab colors of American Dippers can make them difficult to find, but this continuous dipping is a helpful way to locate and identify them.

BIZARRE BIRD FACT: American Dippers can build their nests behind waterfalls. The birds must fly through the waterfall to get in and out.

American Goldfinch

• • ● • •

PRONUNCIATION: *gold-finch*
RANGE: Southern Canada, northern Mexico,
and throughout the United States
HABITAT: Primarily woodlands
FOOD: Seeds
VOICE: High-pitched trills, *po-la-to-chip*

American Goldfinches are tiny yellow birds that are very common to North America. The females and males have different plumage patterns. Female goldfinches are pale yellow all over with black wings and white wing bars. In the spring and summer, males can be identified by their unmistakably yellow body feathers and contrasting black wings with white wing bars. This bird is a frequent visitor to backyard feeders that offer seeds. They will gladly hang around sock feeders filled with nyjer (pronounced *ni-jer*) seeds or pick through spilled sunflower seeds on a platform feeder. When they are perched, their short, notched tails are visible. To identify the tiny bird on the wing, look for their bouncy flight pattern and listen for their lively *"po-ta-to-chip"* flight call.

Goldfinches that spend their summers in southern Canada will migrate to the southern half of the United States and Mexico for the winter, whereas goldfinches that live in the northern half of the United States will remain there all year long. American Goldfinches are found in weedy fields, grasslands, woodlands, and gardens.

While other birds will eat a combination of seeds, berries, and insects, American Goldfinches have an exclusively plant-based diet. Their strong, cone-shaped bills are made especially for cracking open seeds. When foraging, goldfinches will hang from stems of plants to inspect for seeds.

BIZARRE BIRD FACT: American Goldfinches build their nests much later than other songbirds. The goldfinches will wait until mid- to late summer when seeds—their main food source—are abundant.

American Kestrel

······

PRONUNCIATION: *kes-trill*
RANGE: From Alaska and northern Canada
to southern Mexico
HABITAT: Grasslands, deserts, parks
FOOD: Small rodents, snakes, bats, small birds, insects
VOICE: *Klee klee klee*

American Kestrels are the tiniest falcons in North America—they are about the same size as Mourning Doves. They are also one of the most colorful falcons. Female and male kestrels look very similar but are easy to tell apart since males are more colorful. They have reddish-brown backs with black bars, blue-gray wings, light brown chests and bellies with black spots, and black tails. Females have brown feathers with black bars over most of their bodies, and their bellies are white with light brown streaks. Both males and females have the famous kestrel helmet. Their mostly gray heads have black streaks at the corners of their eyes, white patches beneath their eyes and on their chins, and a brown patch on the back of their heads. The feather pattern looks like an ancient battle helmet made specially for the kestrel.

Although they have little bodies, they have big attitudes. American Kestrels are fierce hunters. They patiently sit at the tops of trees or utility poles and scan for prey in open fields with short grass. In areas without poles or trees to perch on, kestrels can hover over a field and scan for food—a skill that no other falcons have. Mice, praying mantis, snakes, moles, frogs, crickets, and small birds are all on the menu. While they are not picky eaters, it may take a while for a bird to notice anything worth eating. You can tell when their keen vision has picked something out to catch when they begin bobbing their head and wagging their tail. The kestrel will then swoop from its perch and pin the prey to the ground with its sharp talons.

Natural landscape features like tree hollows and old wood-pecker holes make perfect nest cavities for kestrels, although they sometimes have to compete with other animals including blue-birds, starlings, and squirrels for the space. Sometimes, the other animals are already living in the nesting cavity but will be kicked out by a kestrel that wants to live there.

BIZARRE BIRD FACT: The feathers on the back of their head make it seem like the American Kestrel has another face.

American Robin

• • ● • •

PRONUNCIATION: *rob-inn*
RANGE: Throughout North America
HABITAT: Forests, woodlands, open fields
FOOD: Insects, berries
VOICE: *Chip! Cheerio! Cheery me!*

American Robins have black heads with small white circles around their eyes, dark brown backs, orange bellies, and white rumps. They have bright yellow bills and brown legs. Male and female robins look nearly the same, but female robins have more white streaks on their throats. Juvenile robins can look as if they are a totally different species. They are much less vibrant compared to adult robins. As youngsters, robins have brown heads and bodies, pale orange sides, and white necks and bellies that are dotted with black spots.

American Robins perform long-lasting musical selections that are rather loud. This early bird is often the first to begin the morning chorus of birdsong. *"Chip! Cheerio! Cheery me!"* sing the robins as they sit at the tops of tall trees. Male robins searching for mates will sing their loudest and longest musical selections in the spring. While both male and female robins sing, they are much less chatty in the fall and nearly silent through the winter.

In spring and summer, American Robins are easily found looking for berries and insects in yards, gardens, fields, shrublands, and forests. American Robins will tilt their heads to get a better look at what's on the ground to eat. When they spot something tasty, they pounce and then jab the ground with their bills, using their strong legs to steady themselves while wrestling out worms stuck in the soil.

Female American Robins build cup-shaped nests made of mud and twigs. These are often tucked away in trees or shrubs, although the craftiest of robins will build nests on the light fixtures or gutters of buildings. The female robin will lay three to five light blue eggs.

BIZARRE BIRD FACT: Migrating robins can fly around 3,000 miles (4,828 km) to reach their destinations. The long-distance flyers are mostly robins that spent their summers in Canada and Alaska. While some robins can travel far between seasons, others choose to stay in one area year-round.

American Three-toed Woodpecker

● ● ● ● ● ●

PRONUNCIATION: *wood-peck-ur*
RANGE: Throughout most of Canada and Alaska,
in portions of the northwestern United States
HABITAT: Coniferous forests and mixed forests
FOOD: Insect larvae, beetles, spiders, tree sap
VOICE: *Pwik pwick*, fast to slow drumming against trees

American Three-toed Woodpeckers are black-and-white-feathered woodpeckers with—you guessed it—three toes on each foot. Their necks and bellies are mostly white, their sides have black and white bars, their backs are mostly white with black spots, and their wings are mostly black with some white spots. Males have a yellow patch of feathers on their heads, while females are all black and white.

To identify these woodpeckers in flight, look for their bouncy flight pattern. You'll find this bird living in forests that have many old and dying trees filled with insect larvae.

Typically, woodpeckers have X-shaped feet with two toes facing forward and two toes facing backward; however, American

Three-toed Woodpeckers are missing one of their back toes. For this bird, having three toes isn't so bad. In fact, missing a toe actually helps them peck at trees harder. These woodpeckers mainly eat grubs that live in tree bark. Considering they eat thousands of insects every day, they are some of the best pest-control solutions a forest can have!

BIZARRE BIRD FACT: American Three-toed Woodpeckers are one of three woodpecker species in the world that have three toes on each foot. The other two species—the Black-backed Woodpecker and Eurasian Three-toed Woodpecker—are closely related to them.

Baltimore Oriole

• • ● • ▲ •

PRONUNCIATION: *or-ee-ole*
RANGE: Central and eastern United States
HABITAT: Open woodlands
FOOD: Berries, oranges, caterpillars, spiders, beetles
VOICE: Short, flutelike whistling

Baltimore Orioles are medium-size songbirds with stunning plumage. Female and male Baltimore Orioles look very different, but each have their own unique beauty. Females have brownish-gray feathers on their heads, backs, and wings, then yellowish-orange feathers on their throats, bellies, and tails. Males have solid black heads and black wings with white barring. They also have bright orange feathers on their chests, bellies, and other tail feathers. Their color patterns almost look like they are ready to celebrate Halloween all year!

This oriole has a black beak that meets at a fine point, which is perfect for eating insects like wasps, caterpillars, mealworms, moths, and grasshoppers. Bird feeders that offer seeds will not attract orioles because these birds have a sweet tooth. So, if you want to bring them to your backyard, set out treats like grape jelly, oranges, and sugar water. Baltimore Orioles will also sip nectar from flowers, so planting nectar-producing native plants around your home is another way to draw them in. The birds get a snack and pollinate your flowers at the same time!

In the summer, Baltimore Orioles are common backyard birds in the central and eastern United States. During the winter, large flocks of orioles gather together and migrate south to Mexico and Central and South America. Once spring rolls around, the orioles will migrate north again to build nests and raise a family.

BIZARRE BIRD FACT: Baltimore Orioles (and other orioles) build large, drooping nests that hang high up on tree branches. The nests are woven together with grass, fur, moss, string, grapevines, and tree bark. It takes about one week for the female to construct the complicated nest. The nest is so well built that the orioles can reuse it the following year.

Black-billed Magpie

• • • • • •

PRONUNCIATION: *mag-pie*
RANGE: From southern Alaska to
midwestern United States
HABITAT: Grasslands, meadows, barnyards, landfills
FOOD: Small mammals, fruit, nuts, insects, carrion, trash
VOICE: Nasally *wok-wok-a-wok*, harsh chattering

Black-billed Magpies are very social relatives of Blue Jays, American Crows, and Common Ravens. Much like their relatives, Black-billed Magpies are incredibly intelligent and strikingly beautiful. Both females and males have the same crisp feather patterns. Their heads, throats, and necks are black. Their shoulders, bellies, and wing tips are white, and their long tail feathers and wings are glossy bluish-green. Depending on the lighting, these glossy feathers can appear to have dark blue, purple, and green streaks, or they can appear all black. The tail feathers are over half the length of their entire body and have a diamond shape when fully spread.

These noisy birds are usually found sitting on the tops of trees or fences in groups. In the winter, up to 200 birds will roost together.

Their communal living strategy works like a home surveillance system. It allows the magpies to always have multiple birds watching for predators in every direction. Should a hawk or other predator enter their territory, the magpies will gang up on the intruder. This behavior is called *mobbing*. Other corvids, like crows and jays, will similarly mob predators until the threat has left the territory. This group effort is especially helpful because the magpies' long tails can get in the way when trying to escape a predator. Working together as a family unit is a proven strategy to keep these birds safe.

Magpies are prone to eat almost anything. Their diet consists of fruit, insects, eggs, small mammals, carrion, and even garbage. Although they are skilled hunters, they are eager to steal food from coyotes or pick at roadkill. They are also known to land on the backs of moose and deer to pick ticks off their hides. Black-billed Magpies can be attracted to home feeders with whole peanuts and suet.

They live year-round in their range, and if you notice this bird near where you live, there is a chance you may be able to find the nest. Together they build their homes at the tops of tall trees, abandoned buildings, or utility poles. The dome-shaped nest is made of twigs, and the inside is lined with mud and grass.

BIZARRE BIRD FACT: Black-billed Magpies get very attached to other magpies. Should a "friend" of theirs die, the magpies will hold a funeral of sorts for their dearly departed. Flocks of up to 40 birds have been observed spending a few minutes mourning next to the body of their fallen friend.

Black-capped Chickadee

•••••

PRONUNCIATION: *chick-a-dee*
RANGE: Southern Canada and the northern United States
HABITAT: Coniferous forests and mixed forests
FOOD: Seeds, insects
VOICE: A nasally *chick-a-dee-dee*

The Black-capped Chickadee is a very tiny songbird that weighs less than a triple-A battery. To identify this chickadee, look for a black head with a white patch on the cheeks and a black throat. They have light brown bellies and light gray backs with dark gray feathers and tails. All these features are sandwiched between a pointy black bill and twiglike black legs.

You'll find this chickadee in the forest in southern Canada and the northern United States, moving quickly from branch to branch as they pluck insects and seeds from the leaves. They move about the tree canopy like miniature gymnasts and are often seen hanging upside down when inspecting even the flimsiest of branches.

Black-capped Chickadees also like to hang out at backyard bird feeders that provide seeds.

These chickadees are built extra hardy to survive very cold winters. Their fluffy feathers act like a puffy jacket to keep them warm. Staying warm, especially at night, requires a lot of energy. Instead of using their stored fat as a source of energy, these chickadees can lower their body temperature to be closer to the temperature outside. This habit is called *torpor* and is similar to hibernation but lasts a much shorter time. It can be difficult to find food in the winter, so, in the fall, Black-capped Chickadees stash bugs and seeds under the edges of tree bark and lichen, securing them by using their saliva as glue.

There are six other kinds of chickadees that call different parts of North America home: the Boreal Chickadee, Carolina Chickadee, Mountain Chickadee, Gray-headed Chickadee, Mexican Chickadee, and Chestnut-backed Chickadee. Most are very commonly seen at backyard bird feeders.

BIZARRE BIRD FACT: Black-capped Chickadees can grow and shrink their brains! During the winter, the memory area of their brain grows 30 percent larger. They need this expansion so they can remember all the places they stored food. Their brains shrink back down in the spring.

Blue Jay

• • ● • •

PRONUNCIATION: *bloo jay*
RANGE: Throughout southern Canada and
the eastern United States
HABITAT: Forests and woodlands
FOOD: Insects, nuts, acorns, eggs
VOICE: *Jeer* and harsh screeches

Blue Jays have (unsurprisingly) blue heads with a crest of pointed feathers, white necks with a black ring, white bellies, and blue backs with white bars.

If you live around Blue Jays, then you have probably noticed how noisy they can be. Blue Jays are very vocal and can produce a variety of calls. Many sound like harsh screeches and metallic squeaks. One of their most notable calls sounds like the bird is shouting "*jeer*"! Along with their variety of squeaks, whistles, and croaks, they are also able to imitate the calls of Red-shouldered and Red-tailed Hawks and Bald Eagles as a way to alert other birds that a predator is nearby. Blue Jays make the most ruckus when they are away from their nest so as to not draw extra attention to their babies.

Blue Jays are commonly found in forests and around gardens where they search for insects to eat. Jays also have an appetite for eggs. They will search trees and bushes for the nests of other birds and will readily eat any unsupervised eggs. Blue Jays are easily attracted to bird feeders. Shelled peanuts are one of their favorite snacks. The jays will gobble several peanuts and store them in a special pouch hidden in their throats. They will then take their nuts to a secret stash spot and store them to eat in the winter. When Blue Jays flock to a bird feeder, they will push aside the smaller birds. Blue Jays' hawk imitations will also scare away other birds from the food. Once the other birds ditch the buffet, the Blue Jays can swoop in and hog the feeder.

BIZARRE BIRD FACT: Blue Jays will pick up ants using their bills and wipe the ants on their feathers. This interesting behavior is called *anting,* and scientists are not entirely sure why Blue Jays do it. Some people think it helps clean the birds' feathers, soothe their skin, or kill parasites.

Burrowing Owl

• • • • • •

PRONUNCIATION: *burro-ing ow-ul*
RANGE: From southern Canada to southern Mexico
HABITAT: Open grasslands, farmlands, airports
FOOD: Insects, small mammals, reptiles
VOICE: *Coo-coooo*, rattle-like hissing

The Burrowing Owl is a small owl that lives in tunnels underground, just like their name says. Burrowing Owls are mostly brown with white dots all over their bodies. The white and brown feather pattern on their faces makes it look as if Burrowing Owls are wearing glasses around their large yellow eyes. Their lanky legs are perfect for running, hopping, digging, and capturing prey like grasshoppers. When flying, Burrowing Owls stay close to the ground. To find food, these owls will hover 30 feet (9 m) off the ground and then dive at something that interests them. They are agile enough to catch prey while in the air.

Burrowing Owls will take over abandoned tunnels dug by animals like prairie dogs and ground squirrels. If no burrows are available, they can dig their own using their long featherless legs and sturdy beaks. The burrows dug by these owls can be up to 10 feet (3 m) long, but the process may take several days. During breeding season, they will build their nests far in the back of the burrow for safety.

Not every owl is a night owl. Burrowing Owls are quite active when the sun is still up, but they also spend hours hunting through the night. Burrowing Owls also differ from other owls because they are very social. They live in colonies that can have hundreds of resident Burrowing Owls across miles of underground tunnels. Burrowing Owls have asymmetrical ears. This means one ear is located high on one side of their skull and the other ear is located low on the other side of their skull. This strange setup gives them superb hearing abilities.

BIZARRE BIRD FACT: When bothered, Burrowing Owls will stand straight up, then take a bow and continue to bob up and down many times. Cowboys gave these owls the nickname "Howdy Birds" because of this interesting bobbing salutation. To ranch hands, the head-bobbing owls looked like they were nodding their heads to say, "Howdy, partner!"

California Quail

· · ● · ·

PRONUNCIATION: *kw-ale*
RANGE: From southern British Columbia
to northwestern Mexico
HABITAT: Deserts, grasslands, backyards
FOOD: Seeds, berries, insects
VOICE: Three-syllable *Chi-ca-go* call, *pit-pit-pit* alarm calls

The California Quail is an adorably plump bird with a ponytail of feathers atop their heads. Their round bodies are decorated with elaborate bands and streaks of gray, brown, yellow, black, and white feathers. Female and male California Quail look slightly different from each other. Both adult birds have dark gray necks, upper chests, and tails, and their lower chest and bellies have white feathers that are thinly outlined with dark brown edges. Their wings are brown with white streaks, and the feathers under their tails are streaked with dark brown and light brown. The main difference between the sexes can be seen in their faces. Females have grayish-brown heads and flat, short ponytails that only stick up about

⅓ inch (1 cm). Male California Quail faces are almost entirely black with bold white streaks above their eyes and around their cheeks. Their decorative crest is over 1 inch (2.5 cm) long and is shaped like a teardrop.

California Quail have stout chicken-like bodies with muscular legs. Like other quail found in North America, the California Quail prefers running over flying. Groups of quail can be found running through or digging in backyards, deserts, and brushy landscapes on the west coast. Approach groups of quail cautiously. If the birds sense danger, they will run away or leave together in an abrupt flight, called *flushing*. The hope is that potential predators will be too stunned by the explosion of quail and unable to grab a bird to eat.

In the winter, California Quail gather into large groups of up to 70 birds. These groups, called *coveys,* help protect against predators when they go foraging for food. The coveys are also able to huddle together on chilly nights to stay warm. When spring returns, the coveys will disband as males and females pair off for the breeding season.

California Quail love taking dust baths. They will use their strong legs to scrape the ground and then will lower their bodies into the loosened bowl of dirt. The quail will wiggle around, rubbing their heads and bodies to get an even coating of dust all over. The dust helps their feathers stay healthy.

BIZARRE BIRD FACT: The California Quail is the state bird of California.

Carolina Wren

• • ● • •

PRONUNCIATION: *ren*
RANGE: Northern and eastern Mexico,
throughout the eastern United States
HABITAT: Woodlands, shrubby fields, gardens
FOOD: Seeds, insects
VOICE: Buzzy trilling, *tea-kettle tea-kettle tea-kettle,*
cheery cheery cheery

Carolina Wrens are small yet energetic birds that are likely to be seen in yards and parks throughout the eastern United States. These wrens have reddish-brown feathers on their heads and backs, a white stripe just above their eyes, white throats, and light brown bellies. They have an interesting silhouette—their large heads support a long, slender bill that curves downward and from their plump bodies sprouts a long, stiff tail that often sticks straight up.

Find this wren rapidly hopping across the ground or swiftly climbing tangled vines and tree branches. The main diet of the

Carolina Wren includes insects like caterpillars, beetles, and grasshoppers. They use their pointed bills to probe crevices and flip through leaf litter. It can be hard to spot wrens because they quickly dodge in and out of thick shrubs. While catching a good glimpse of a wren can be challenging, hearing them is far easier. Adult wrens commonly travel in pairs that sing and call all year long to defend their territory. Only male Carolina Wrens sing the *"tea-kettle tea-kettle tea-kettle"* and *"cheery cheery cheery"* songs. Female wrens make a chattering trill call. Together the male and female will perform a duet that seamlessly combines their songs and calls into one musical phrase. Carolina Wrens will sing all day long. A male Carolina Wren was once recorded singing 3,000 times in one day.

BIZARRE BIRD FACT: Carolina Wrens will nest in the most unexpected places—from mailboxes and tires to old shoes and jacket pockets.

Common Raven

•••••

PRONUNCIATION: *ray-ven*
RANGE: Throughout Alaska, Canada, and Mexico
as well as the western and northeastern United States
HABITAT: Almost anywhere,
except Great Plains and Southeast Forests
FOOD: Insects, rodents, berries, birds, seeds,
nuts, eggs, carrion
VOICE: Croaking, bubbling, popping

Common Ravens are large, elegant, and intelligent birds. They can be found in almost any habitat in North America including beaches, tundras, mountains, and deserts where they will live year-round. For centuries people around the world have been fascinated by how smart, playful, and sometimes creepy ravens can be. Because of their long history with humans, many myths, poems, stories, and folktales exist about ravens.

Common Ravens are *omnivores,* meaning they eat everything including meat and plants. They will commonly eat dead animals they find and are also known to hunt birds and rodents. The ravens have a special pouch in their throats where they can store food to eat later.

Ravens and crows look very similar to each other, but they are not the same birds. They are both related and belong to a group of birds called corvids. Other corvids you may be familiar with include Blue Jays and Black-billed Magpies. Since crows and ravens can live in the same regions, it's important to understand how to tell them apart. Get to know some of the differences between ravens and crows:

- Ravens are very large birds, standing almost 2 feet tall (0.6 m) with a 5-foot (1.5-m) wingspan. Their long flight feathers extend like wispy fingers from the tips of their wings. Crows, on the other hand, are much smaller, standing about 17 inches (43.2 cm) with 3-foot (1-m) wingspans.

- Ravens have long feathers growing on top of their very thick bills and long, shaggy neck feathers. Crows have shorter feathers growing on thin bills and no flowy neck feathers.

- Ravens have long, diamond-shaped tails. Crows have short, square-shaped tails. The length and shape of their tails are best seen during flight and are the easiest way to identify a crow or raven.

- Ravens and crows have very different vocalizations. Ravens make grumbly croaking sounds and crows *caw-caw-caw*.

BIZARRE BIRD FACT: Ravens are excellent mimics and can imitate human speech better than parrots.

Dark-eyed Junco

• • • • • •

PRONUNCIATION: *jun-co*
RANGE: From northern Canada to northern Mexico
HABITAT: Primarily dry, semiopen scrublands
FOOD: Insects, seeds, berries
VOICE: Loud, high-pitched chips

Dark-eyed Juncos are small birds related to sparrows. Although they're typically gray with pink bills and pink legs, they can look different depending on where they are from. That's right! Dark-eyed Juncos have various feather patterns based on the region where they live. In fact, the variations are so extreme that they sometimes look like completely different birds. Birders jokingly call these regional variations *flavors*. There are six flavors of junco spread across North America: Slate-colored, Oregon, Pink-sided, Gray-headed, White-winged, and Red-backed. In the North Pacific Coast region, Dark-eyed Juncos are of the Oregon flavor. These juncos have dark heads, white bellies, and white feathers on the outsides of their tails. A bird guide can help you determine which Dark-eyed Junco lives in your region.

Dark-eyed Juncos spend their summers throughout much of Canada where they breed in forests with shrubby understories. They will migrate to the fields and forests of the United States and northern Mexico for the winter months. Dark-eyed Juncos travel in flocks made of multiple bird species including sparrows, kinglets, and chickadees. They all work together to find food and stay safe from predators until spring arrives. The flocks can commonly be found foraging in lawns, at feeders, on trails, and on the forest floor. You can tell Dark-eyed Juncos apart from the rest of the flock by checking for the white feathers on the outside of their tails as they fly.

BIZARRE BIRD FACT: Dark-eyed Juncos are one of the most common bird species in North America.

Downny Woodpecker

• • ● • • •

PRONUNCIATION: *dow-knee wood-peck-ur*
RANGE: Throughout Canada and the United States
HABITAT: Forests and woodlands
FOOD: Insects
VOICE: Laughing, horselike whinny, *pik pik*

Downy Woodpeckers are tiny woodpeckers that are found year-round in woodlands in both urban and rural areas throughout Canada and the United States. Their bellies are all white, their wings are black with small white spots, and on their backs sits a big white patch of feathers. They have a black stripe on their crowns, behind their eyes, and behind their bills like a fancy mustache. White patches fill in between the black markings on their faces. Females and males look quite similar, but the main difference is that males have a small patch of red feathers on the backs of their heads. Downy Woodpeckers have very short bills. The length of their bills is shorter than the length of their heads. This tip is useful when telling Downy Woodpeckers apart from Hairy Woodpeckers.

While the plumage of a Hairy Woodpecker is nearly identical to that of the Downy Woodpecker, the bills of Hairy Woodpeckers are longer than their heads.

Downy Woodpeckers are specialized for living in trees. Using their pointed bills like a hammer and chisel, woodpeckers drill holes into wood to find beetles, ants, and larvae. Downy Woodpeckers will poke at thin branches and tear away bark along tree trunks to find food. They also have extremely long tongues with tiny but sharp hooks at the end that grab onto insects hidden in trees. The Downy Woodpecker tongue is so long that it wraps around the woodpecker's brain! Considering they eat thousands of insects every day, they are some of the best pest-control solutions a forest can have. They also use their bills to dig deep nesting cavities in trees.

These woodpeckers have short and stiff feathers that cover their nostrils and protect the birds from sawdust and chips of wood. They also have special feet to help them grab onto vertical surfaces like tree trunks: X-shaped feet with two toes facing forward and two toes facing backward.

BIZARRE BIRD FACT: Downy Woodpeckers can be identified by the sound of their bills tapping against trees. Their tapping, also called *drumming*, is used to communicate with nearby woodpeckers. Another way you can tell what species of woodpecker is around is looking at the shape and pattern of the holes left in trees.

Eastern Bluebird

• • •• • •

PRONUNCIATION: *bloo-bird*
RANGE: From California to Louisiana
and southward to central Mexico
HABITAT: Open, grassy fields
FOOD: Insects, berries
VOICE: *Tchew dweedee*

Eastern Bluebirds and their colorful appearance bring smiles to people all throughout North America. Bluebirds arrive in the northern parts of their home range in early spring. For this reason, many people relate bluebirds to springtime festivities, happiness, and hope. In the winter, Eastern Bluebirds spend their time in northern Mexico. Not all Eastern Bluebirds migrate, however. If the birds can reliably find food and shelter, they are less likely to relocate when the seasons change. A good number of bluebirds call parts of central Mexico and the southeastern United States home all year long.

The dazzling blue and orange feathers of Eastern Bluebirds make them very easy to identify. Bluebirds have blue feathers on their heads, backs, and tails. Their throat and chest feathers are orange, and their bellies are white. Male and female Eastern Bluebirds look slightly different from one another—the feathers of male bluebirds are intensely colored while the females' coloration is not as bold.

Eastern Bluebirds are best found in places that have open fields and a few scattered trees. Parks, farmlands, and cemeteries are good examples of places to find Eastern Bluebirds. They like to perch on branches and fences while they wait for a tasty insect to fly by.

Bluebirds like to build nests inside of hollow tree holes. Male Eastern Bluebirds let nearby female bluebirds know that they've found a nice place to build a nest by sitting atop the tree and waving their bright blue wings side to side, hoping to get their attention.

In the 1920s, Eastern Bluebirds lost a serious amount of their habitat due to deforestation. Without trees, they were unable to build nests and raise their young. Bluebirds went from being commonly found to rarely found in just a few decades. Concerned bird lovers started campaigns to help them by building nest boxes. The nest boxes imitated natural tree cavities and gave bluebirds somewhere else to construct their nests. Thankfully, this campaign was very successful and helped Eastern Bluebirds become a commonly found bird again.

BIZARRE BIRD FACT: Did you know the blue color in bird feathers is an optical illusion? Blue is not a naturally occurring feather color. It is created when natural light passes through them. A blue feather held in sunlight looks blue, but a blue feather held in the shade looks brown.

Eastern Wood-Pewee

· · ● · · ·

PRONUNCIATION: *pee-wee*
RANGE: From southeastern Canada through southeastern Mexico, as well as California to Louisiana and southward to central Mexico
HABITAT: Forests, woodlands, forest edges
FOOD: Insects
VOICE: *Pee-a-wee, wee-ooo*

Eastern Wood-Pewees are small grayish-brown birds with white chests, white bars on their wings, and a small yellow patch on the bottom of their bellies. Their simple appearance can be confused with a few other birds that look similar, but Eastern Wood-Pewees have a unique call. Male pewees sing out their name in a musical tone that livens up the forests they spend their summers in.

Pewees are part of a group of birds called *flycatchers*. Like their name states, flycatchers eat flies and other insects as their main food. They are mostly found in woodlands and forest edges throughout eastern North America. Their diet includes moths, dragonflies, bees, crickets, and flies. They like to perch on dead tree branches where they watch for insects. When pewees find their prey, they will dart from their perch, catch the insect, and return to the same perch to eat the bug all in a matter of seconds. The pewee will sit for a few moments while it waits to grab another passing bug. This hunting habit is unique to flycatchers and is a helpful tip for identifying Eastern Wood-Pewees.

BIZARRE BIRD FACT: Eastern Wood-Pewees have a west coast twin called the Western Wood-Pewee. The two birds look identical but sound very different from one another.

European Starling

• • • • • •

PRONUNCIATION: *star-ling*
RANGE: Throughout North America
HABITAT: Fields, cities, towns
FOOD: Grasshoppers, beetles, berries, seeds, trash
VOICE: Mimicked sounds, whistles, trills

European Starlings are small black birds that are considered one of the most abundant bird species in the world. All you need is a quick glance to know what you're seeing is a starling. Both males and females have glossy black plumage that shimmers green and purple in the sunlight. They have short, squared tails, pointed wings, and a long, pointed bill. In flight, starlings are shaped like triangular tortilla chips. Female and male starlings can be told apart by the faint colors found at the base of their yellow bills. Males have a bluish spot at the base of their bills, while females sport a pinkish spot.

European Starlings are native to Europe and Asia but were introduced to North America in 1890. They are found in most places that humans occupy—neighborhoods, city streets, parks, farms, fields, and shopping malls. The European Starling's diet is made up of insects, seeds, fruit, and trash. For much of the year, they wheel through the sky and mob places where food is abundant. They are commonly found foraging sports fields, parking lots, and yards. The starlings will stab their long, sharp bills into the ground to search for grubs and will also visit platform bird feeders.

During the winter, you may be lucky enough to see a starling murmuration form over the birds' communal roosting site—where birds meet up to sleep. A *murmuration* is a mesmerizing sky dance preformed in unison by a flock of birds. These flocks gather in the evening and perform amazing aerobatic displays. They will fly in a continuously changing formation before dropping into their roosting sites. Sleeping in a large group provides safety in numbers.

European Starlings have an amazing ability to mimic the calls of other birds, human speech, and other animals. Male and female starlings can be heard throughout the year combining their high-pitched trills and whistles with mimicked sounds.

BIZARRE BIRD FACT: The classical composer Wolfgang Amadeus Mozart owned a pet starling that inspired some of his music.

Golden Eagle

••●••

PRONUNCIATION: *ee-gull*
RANGE: Throughout North America
HABITAT: Grasslands, mountain ranges, deserts
FOOD: Rabbits, squirrels, foxes, coyotes, deer
VOICE: Whistling screeches

Golden Eagles are hefty yet agile birds that have shiny golden feathers on the backs of their heads and necks and also under their tails. These feathers are not exactly dipped in gold, but they are golden brown and stand out against the rest of the bird's plumage. This bird of prey is similar to Bald Eagles, but Golden Eagles are slightly larger and are covered with dark brown feathers. Golden Eagles are one of the few raptors with feathers covering their entire legs. Their bright yellow feet and deadly talons poke out of the bottoms of their feathery pants.

They can be found all over the continent but are most reliably seen in the western half of North America. They live in all kinds of habitats including deserts, grasslands, mountain ranges, canyons, and hillsides. The only places they will certainly avoid are busy cities.

These big birds have even bigger appetites and will hunt large animals like wolves, deer, seals, geese, cows, and bobcats! However, smaller prey like squirrels, mice, rabbits, grasshoppers, and fish are also on the menu. Their eyes have super-sharp vision that lets them clearly see things over a mile away. Once the eagle's eyes lock onto prey, there is little chance for escape. Golden Eagles hunt while soaring and dive from above at incredible speeds to slam their prey to the ground. Sometimes Golden Eagles will scavenge for carrion and steal eggs from bird nests.

BIZARRE BIRD FACT: Golden Eagles are the national bird of Mexico and are pictured on the country's flag. Four other countries around the world have also claimed the Golden Eagle as their official national symbol.

Gray Catbird

......

PRONUNCIATION: *cat-bird*
RANGE: From southern Canada to the Gulf of Mexico
HABITAT: Shrublands and viny forest edges
FOOD: Insects, berries
VOICE: Sings a collection of continuous squeaks, whistles, catlike mews, and parts of other birds' songs with occasional pauses

Gray Catbirds are medium-size songbirds that have short wings and long, rounded tails. They are mostly gray all over except for their black crowns, black tails, and rusty brown undertail feathers. The pop of color underneath their tails can best be seen when they are flying. You'll also notice their distinctly rounded tails best when they're flying, but the shape is visible when they are perched as well. Their bills are solid black, and they stand on long grayish-black legs.

This bird can usually be found in dense shrubs, vines, and thickets along woodlands. They move through the matrix of plants using a combination of hopping and short flights. When perched, their tails hang stiffly downward. These tails occasionally bounce while they are communicating.

Gray Catbirds are talented singers thanks to their *syrinx,* a two-sided organ in their chest that is similar to human vocal cords. Catbirds can control each side of their syrinx separately, which allows them to sing two different notes at the same time. They are related to other talented songbirds like Northern Mockingbirds and Brown Thrashers, all of which are very good at mimicking sounds. Catbirds will listen, learn, and imitate the songs and calls of birds found living near their territory. Gray Catbirds will loudly flaunt their musical abilities atop bushes and trees. They can sing over 100 different sounds for 10 straight minutes without taking a break!

BIZARRE BIRD FACT: The name *catbird* comes from the catlike mewing calls these birds include in their songs.

Great Black-backed Gull

• • • • • •

PRONUNCIATION: *guh-l*
RANGE: Shorelines along eastern North America
HABITAT: Beaches, shorelines
FOOD: Fish, birds, mammals, carrion, trash
VOICE: Loud squawking, high-pitched screeches

Great Black-backed Gulls are large seagulls that live on the eastern coast of North America from Labrador to Florida. They have crisp white heads, necks, and bellies, with dark gray backs and wings. While this gull looks very similar to most other seagulls, the Great Black-backed is massive in comparison. They are one of the largest gulls in the world and are skilled predators that sit at the top of the food chain. Great Black-backed Gulls are opportunistic hunters that will prey on mammals, fish, eggs, carrion, and other birds. They can develop a special appetite for newly hatched shorebird chicks. Although they are great hunters, they will also eat scraps of food left in streets, dumpsters, and parking lots. They will even steal food from other birds and beachgoers.

Many birders would consider this gull a "trash bird" because they are very common and abundant—and they also love trash. But eating trash and being very common shouldn't take away from the Great Black-backed Gulls' beauty. Besides, their trash-eating habit is a service that deserves more praise than it gets.

Flip through the gull section of any birding field guide and you will find photos of black-and-white birds that all look and sound similar. As if adult seagulls were not enough of a headache to tell apart, young seagulls can be even more difficult to identify. Younger gulls have yearly molts that change their feather patterns and bill colors. The younger birds are checkered with brown and white feathers. It takes four years for Great Black-backed Gulls to molt into their final black and white plumage.

BIZARRE BIRD FACT: Seagulls stand on one leg as a way to keep their feet warm. Their hidden leg is tucked into their feathers and held close to their body.

Great Blue Heron

• • ● • •

PRONUNCIATION: *hair-ron*
RANGE: Throughout North America
HABITAT: Wetlands, ponds, shallow rivers, coastlines
FOOD: Fish, snakes, rodents
VOICE: Croaking *awk-awk*, raspy *roh-roh-roh*

The Great Blue Heron is a massive bird with long legs and an even longer neck. They are mostly blush-gray but have white patches on their faces and dark blue patches near their "armpits," on the tips of their wings, and at the tops of their heads. (The area under a bird's wing analogous to our armpits is known as the *axillary*.) Long, pointed feathers elegantly hang from their necks and backs. You have probably seen this bird standing very still in shallow water. Their long legs let them wade across ponds, slow rivers, coastlines, and all kinds of waters throughout North America. They will move slowly through the water while hunting so as not to scare the fish, frogs, and snakes swimming nearby. Herons strike with lightning-quick speed to stab their prey with their sharp yellow bills. Their neck muscles are specially aligned to keep them from getting whiplash. Herons then swallow their catch whole.

Great Blue Herons come in an all-white variety that is commonly found in Florida. These are called Great White Herons, and they look like the giant version of another common waterbird: the Great Egret. Look for the heron's long neck feathers and pale legs. The Great Egret does not have long neck feathers, and its legs are black.

Great Blue Herons also look like cranes but, obviously, are not the same bird. You can tell herons and cranes apart by looking at their necks. Herons have S-shaped necks that stay deeply bent while the birds are flying and standing. Cranes will stick their necks straight out while flying and just slightly bend them while standing.

BIZARRE BIRD FACT: Great Blue Herons have special claws with a built-in comb on their middle toe. The herons comb their feathers to remove built-up oils and fish slime.

Greater Roadrunner

• • •••••

PRONUNCIATION: *road-run-ur*
RANGE: From California to Louisiana and
southward to central Mexico
HABITAT: Primarily dry, semiopen scrublands
FOOD: Scorpions, lizards, snakes,
small mammals, birds, carrion, insects
VOICE: Slow, mournful *co-coo-cooo-coooo*. Their
cooing sounds like a whining puppy. Also makes yipping
sounds that are similar to the sounds of a kazoo.

You may find it surprising to know Greater Roadrunners are a type of cuckoo because they look drastically different from the more familiar species of cuckoo found in North America. Greater Roadrunners are one of the most famous desert-dwelling birds in North America; however, they are not limited to just deserts. They can also be found in pine forests, suburban neighborhoods, and grasslands. Their lesser known relative, aptly named the Lesser Roadrunner, lives in southern Mexico.

Greater Roadrunners are, perhaps, best known for their amazing speed, which allows them to travel quickly from place to place instead of flying. Do you think you can outrun a roadrunner? The average person can run around 7 miles per hour (11.3 kph). Usain Bolt, the fastest human, can sprint at 27 miles per hour (43.5 kph). Greater Roadrunners can reach speeds of around 15 miles per hour (24 kph). So, unless you are a trained athlete or you happen to have a jetpack strapped to you, the Greater Roadrunner will easily win this imaginary race.

They rely on their quick reflexes to help them catch fast-moving prey like scorpions, rattlesnakes, and even hummingbirds! While hunting, roadrunners will sit and scan for tasty morsels to come in view. When potential food is noticed, the roadrunner will pounce on it with great speed. Roadrunners will smash larger food items against rocks to tenderize them before eating.

BIZARRE BIRD FACT: Greater Roadrunners can eat poisonous and venomous prey without being harmed.

House Sparrow

· · ● · · ·

PRONUNCIATION: *spare-row*
RANGE: Throughout North America
HABITAT: Cities and urban environments
FOOD: Seeds, insects, trash
VOICE: Loud chirping

House Sparrows are small, yet very energetic birds found all over North America. You can probably guess by their name that they are frequently found near houses. House Sparrows have a very close relationship with humans. They will happily build their nests in vents, gutters, utility poles, stoplights, and so on. House Sparrows will take up residence alongside humans and use our scraps and trash to build their own kingdoms. Aside from trash, House Sparrows will eat seeds and insects.

House Sparrow females and males look slightly different. The female has a warm brown head, grayish-brown chest and belly, and a back with light brown and dark brown streaks. The male has a gray, brown, and white head with a black chin and throat. The back and belly of the male House Sparrow are very similar to female House Sparrows.

House Sparrows are native to Europe, Asia, and North Africa, but have been introduced to most continents outside of their natural range. The sparrows have become well established in North America, and now over 80 million House Sparrows call this continent their home.

While there are millions of House Sparrows living in North America, their numbers are slowly declining each year. European House Sparrow populations are down nearly 60 percent from their historic numbers. Reduced availability of nesting sites, food sources, and other resources is a big threat to common and specialized bird species alike.

BIZARRE BIRD FACT: House Sparrows can live in some unusual places. They have been found living inside warehouses and stores and have even been found 2,000 feet (610 m) below the ground in a coal mine.

Killdeer

· · ● ● ● ·

PRONUNCIATION: *kill-deer*
RANGE: From northern Canada to southern Mexico
HABITAT: Open fields, farmlands, parks, mudflats
FOOD: Insects
VOICE: *Kill-dee*, trilling

Killdeer are small shorebirds that are more commonly found in grassy parks than on the beach. They have brown backs and wings, rusty rufous tails, white bellies, two black stripes around their necks, and heads with brown, white, and black patches. A thin and bright orange ring around their eyes adds a surprising pop of color to their otherwise earthy appearance.

Killdeer are very noisy and easy to identify just by their calls. Their bizarre name comes from their call, which sounds like the bird is saying "*kill-dee.*" Killdeer calls are high-pitched and repeated many times especially when the bird is alarmed. You will probably hear this bird before you see it.

These birds are very common and can be found everywhere from neighborhood lawns and parking lots to farmlands and mudflats where they spend much of the day searching for insects. Killdeer can make use of pretty much any open area and will also nest in urban areas. They do not need trees to build their nests, which are simply shallow, uncovered bowls dug into the dirt. Unlike many birds, Killdeer chicks are fully feathered and can walk and feed themselves soon after hatching! The chicks even look like fluffy miniature versions of their parents.

BIZARRE BIRD FACT: Killdeer adults will pretend to have a broken wing to distract predators that come too close to their nests and chicks. If you see a killdeer dragging one wing on the ground, there's a chance you're very close to its nest. Walk carefully! Their nests blend in with the ground.

Mississippi Kite

· · ● · · ·

PRONUNCIATION: *kye-t*
RANGE: From the southern United States
to southeastern Mexico
HABITAT: Prairies, wetlands, sports fields
FOOD: Grasshoppers, lizards, frogs, rodents, small birds
VOICE: High-pitched squeaky whistle, *ki-kiii*

Mississippi Kites are small hawks with white heads, black tails, light gray bodies, and gray wings with black tips. They have striking red eyes surrounded by black feathers, delicate black bills, and yellow talons. In flight, notice their triangular black tail, pointed white wings, and white heads to tell these birds of prey from others. You are likely to hear a Mississippi Kite before you actually see it. Their whistling calls sound like a dog toy being squeezed.

Mississippi Kites are talented flyers that can sail, swoop, and dive in the wind just like their namesake toy. Their flight skills combined with their keen eyesight make them perfectly equipped to catch fast-moving insects like grasshoppers, cicadas, and dragonflies. They can catch insects in their talons directly out of the air then eat their catch all while still flying. Groups of kites will follow farmers cutting hayfields to catch the bugs that jump out of the way of tractors.

At the tops of tall trees in parks, golf courses, cemeteries, and similar habitats are where you will find the nests of Mississippi Kites. Unlike other birds of prey, these kites are fairly social and will build their nests close to each other during the breeding season. This strategy helps the birds stay safe and give the nesting adult kites some much-needed assistance caring for their babies. Young kites, around one year old, will offer to help incubate eggs and watch over the nest just like a babysitter. Kites are very territorial of their nests, however. If you happen to find a nesting colony, be sure to give them plenty of space. They are known to dive-bomb intruders.

BIZARRE BIRD FACT: Kites will purposefully place wasp nests in their own nests or build their nest next to one. The stinging insects will not bother the kites but will protect their nests from predators like squirrels and raccoons.

Mourning Dove

•••••

PRONUNCIATION: *morn-ing duh-v*
RANGE: From southern Canada to central Mexico
HABITAT: Almost anywhere, from open areas in
neighborhoods to shrubby natural spaces
FOOD: Grains, seeds, fruit
VOICE: A low frequency *whooeeooo hoo-hoo-hoo*.
Sometimes a single low *cooo*. Their wings make
whistling sounds when flying.

This dove gets its name from the slow, owl-like hoots that make it sound like the bird is mournfully singing. Mourning Doves are medium-size birds with brownish belly feathers and grayish feathers with black dots on the top of their wings. Their tail feathers are mostly white at the bottom and have black tips. They have short pink legs and small heads with a slender black bill. In general, doves do very well living near people. They prefer open areas like lawns and playgrounds but can also be found in shrubby landscapes with some trees. Mourning Doves also like to rest on telephone wires, and you'll often spot them hanging out in a group.

Mourning Doves are extremely common visitors at backyard bird feeders. They are likely to settle on the ground picking up fallen seeds. Doves will pick up more food than they plan to eat in one sitting and store extra grains in a special part of their throat called the *crop*. The crop allows doves to quickly pick up large amounts of food in one place, kind of like a to-go box. They will wait to eat their extra food until they are resting in a safe place. The crop has a bunch of muscles that help doves "chew" their food before digestion. Doves will also swallow small rocks and bits of dirt to assist in breaking up the grains in their crops.

BIZARRE BIRD FACT: Does the Mourning Dove remind you of another popular bird found in cities? If you think they look like pigeons, then you're on the right track! Doves and pigeons are related. The pigeons we most commonly see in North America are domestic Rock Pigeons. You know, the city-dwelling birds that people like to feed in parks. Rock Pigeons share a lot of similarities with Mourning Doves.

Northern Cardinal

······

PRONUNCIATION: *car-di-nal*
RANGE: Found in the eastern United States
and eastern Mexico
HABITAT: Woodlands, gardens, shrublands
FOOD: Seeds, insects
VOICE: *Birdie birdie birdie, Pew pew pew,* loud chipping

Northern Cardinals are common throughout eastern North America. The male cardinal is best known because of his almost entirely red body, red crest, and black mask of feathers around his eyes. Female cardinals are mostly brown but have red feathers on their crests, wings, and tails.

Northern Cardinals are nonmigratory. They will hang out in shrubby fields, lawns, gardens, woodlands, and parks. Once they've found a territory to call their own, they'll stay put and establish home ranges. It's possible that the Northern Cardinals in your neighborhood have had that established home range for years!

Cardinals call and sing frequently to keep in contact with their lifelong mate—another bird that is often milling about a few feet away. Their loud calls pierce the air like laser beams. Listen closely to a cardinal's call and you will hear them *"pew pew pew."*

Cardinals will flock to feeders that are stocked with seeds, especially feeders that have a steady supply of sunflower seeds. Cardinals are equipped with the perfect tool to eat seeds—a chunky, orange, triangular bill that comes to a point. They use their bills like a nutcracker easily opening hard seeds. Northern Cardinals' bold colors come along with a bold personality.

BIZARRE BIRD FACT: The feather color of cardinals—and most other birds with red, orange, and yellow feathers—comes from the foods they eat. Male cardinals that eat red and orange berries become even more vibrant.

Northern Mockingbird

• • ● • •

PRONUNCIATION: *mock-ing-bird*
RANGE: Throughout the United States and Mexico
HABITAT: Open fields, parks, gardens
FOOD: Insects, berries
VOICE: Repeats mimicked phrases two to six times, raspy

Northern Mockingbirds are mostly gray on their heads, backs, and tails but have whitish throats and bellies. In flight, the white feathers lining the outer edges of the tail are visible along with the white patches on the ends of their dark brown wings. Northern Mockingbirds have an expansive range throughout Mexico and the United States. They are generalists, which means they can live in a wide range of habitats. Mockingbirds are found everywhere from lawns to woodlands to deserts. Throughout most of their range, mockingbirds do not migrate. Instead, they are common, year-round residents and are slowly expanding farther north.

Mockingbirds get their name from their ability to imitate, or mock, the sounds around them. Both male and female mocking-birds sing. They can learn hundreds of sounds including the songs of other birds, car alarms, the sounds of frogs or dogs, and construction noise. During the breeding season, males will sing day and night to find a mate and defend their territory.

Even as babies, mockingbirds are skilled at learning songs. They listen to their parents' songs and practice those as best they can. Mockingbirds continue to learn new songs throughout their lives. They will add newly learned songs to their playlist as needed. Mockingbirds are not able to reproduce every sound there is. Some sounds, like trills, are too complex even for this masterful mimic.

BIZARRE BIRD FACT: Northern Mockingbirds will fiercely defend their nests. They are known to dive-bomb anything and everything that wanders too close.

Osprey

· · ● ● · ·

PRONUNCIATION: *oss-pray*
RANGE: Throughout North America
HABITAT: Near open water
FOOD: Fish
VOICE: High-pitched, whistle-like screeches

Ospreys are large eagle-like birds with distinct features. Their backs and the top side of their wings are chocolate brown, the underside of their wings are brown and white, and their bellies are mostly white. Their heads are mostly white, but a brown band of feathers runs across their striking yellow eyes and down the side of their neck. Their silhouette in the sky is unlike any other birds'. The Osprey's long wings appear kinked in the center and their heads are focused downward as they scan the waters below. Their wingbeat is deep and steady in flight, though ospreys will hover when a tasty fish catches their eye.

Ospreys are widely dispersed birds of prey that are found on every continent except Antarctica. They can thrive in areas that have open bodies of water to catch fish, their main food source. Ospreys are often called Fish Hawks or Fish Eagles because 99 percent of their diet is fish.

They are skillful hunters that are very well adapted to catching live fish swimming in shallow water. Even when Ospreys are flying 130 feet (40 m) in the air, they can locate fish swimming in the waters below. Once a fish is targeted, an Osprey will patiently wait for the perfect moment to dive into the water talons first. Their large feet and extremely long talons act like a fishing net with hooks. Ospreys only dive about 3 feet (1 m) into the water and latch onto their prey with an unbreakable grip. They use their powerful wings to lift themselves and their prey out of the water. Once in flight, they can flip the fish to a front-facing position and then fly to a nearby tree to chow down.

BIZARRE BIRD FACT: Ospreys use large sticks to build 4-feet-wide (1.4-m) nests atop trees, cliffs, or human-made nesting platforms. Generations of ospreys can return to the same nest to raise their young year after year.

Ovenbird

••••••

PRONUNCIATION: *ov-en-bird*
RANGE: Throughout most of Canada, Alaska,
and the eastern United States
HABITAT: Shaded forests
FOOD: Insects, berries
VOICE: With increasing in volume,
tea-cher TEA-cher TEA-CHER

Ovenbirds are small and secretive. They have an orange patch on the tops of their brown heads, yellowish-brown backs, and white bellies with black streaks. These birds are a type of warbler that prefer walking on the ground instead of perching on trees like typical warblers. They strut across the forest floor on pink legs and pick up insects with their slender bills. Ovenbird plumage also looks very different compared to other warblers. The warblers that are typically found in trees have yellow, orange, and sometimes blue feathers. Luckily, ovenbirds have brown, black, and white feathers, which help them blend into their surroundings.

Ovenbirds are more likely to be heard first and seen later. They have an enormous voice that fills the forest with beautiful songs. If you've ever ventured into forests in the eastern United States during the summer, you've likely heard the Ovenbird's song. Most birds sing during the daytime to attract mates and defend their territory. Male Ovenbirds will sing whimsical songs day and night. Their unusual nighttime song is paired with a dramatic flight routine.

So what's with their name? The "oven" in question refers to the nest. Female Ovenbirds create nests on the ground in the shape of a domed oven. They construct them from tree bark and grass, then line the inside with animal fur. To hide from predators, they place twigs and leaves from the surrounding area on top of the nest, which makes it look just like the forest floor around it. Ovenbirds will also build a secret side entrance to access the inside of the nest. Ovenbird nests are so well camouflaged that you can walk right past one on a nature trail and never notice it.

BIZARRE BIRD FACT: Female Ovenbirds eat the eggshells of their freshly hatched babies.

Red Crossbill

• • • • • •

PRONUNCIATION: *cross-bill*
RANGE: From southern Alaska to western Mexico
HABITAT: Coniferous forests
FOOD: Cone seeds
VOICE: Musical trilling, *chip-chip-chip*

The Red Crossbill is a small finch-like bird with a very unusual bill. Female Red Crossbills are greenish-yellow with gray spotting and dark brown wings. Male Red Crossbills are brick red, but can sometimes be yellow and have dark brown wings. They get their name from their curiously twisted bills. They twist their beaks between the scales of pine cones before using their tongues to scoop out the yummy seeds hidden inside.

Unlike many other birds, Red Crossbills do not migrate between seasons. They move from place to place depending on how much food is available. Red Crossbills are commonly found throughout Canada, the western United States, and western Mexico but will wander to coniferous forests outside of this range if the cones that are their main food become hard to find. They can travel over 100 miles (161 km) a day in search of food. Crossbills have another unusual ability that sets them apart from most other birds—they're able to lay eggs and raise their young at any time of year—yes, even winter! As long as there are enough cones for the adults and baby birds to eat, crossbills will build their nests.

BIZARRE BIRD FACT: Young crossbill beaks start out straight and begin curving as they grow up. Their beaks can twist to the right or left depending on which way the bird prefers to remove cone seeds.

Rock Pigeon

••••••

PRONUNCIATION: *pij-in*
RANGE: Throughout North America
HABITAT: Cities and urban environments
FOOD: Seeds, insects, trash
VOICE: Cooing

Rock Pigeons are very common birds in urbanized areas. Pigeons will turn any concrete jungle into a place they call home. Typically, they have light gray bodies sandwiched between dark gray heads and tails. On their wings are two black stripes. Look closely at their necks and you will notice shimmering purple and blue feathers. Their bright pink feet are short but sturdy.

Wild pigeons are native to Europe, North Africa, and southwestern Asia and were brought to North America in the 17th century by European colonists who emigrated to the Atlantic coast. The birds can now be found all throughout North America. Can you even recall the last time you were in a city and didn't encounter a pigeon? Their ability to thrive nearly everywhere is partially thanks to the endless heaps of trash humans produce, which then nourish little baby pigeons, and structures like tall buildings and highway overpasses, which support their nests.

Rock Pigeons come in an array of colors and feather types aside from the gray and black variety. Pigeons are kept as pets and are bred for their looks. There are over 800 breeds of domestic pigeons, which leaves plenty of room for some to look absolutely ridiculous—just take a look at the Pouter Pigeon when you get a chance.

BIZARRE BIRD FACT: In the past, pigeons were trained to fly mail from place to place. Letters would be written on a small piece of paper and rolled into a storage tube harnessed to the pigeon.

Rufous Hummingbird

• • • • • •

PRONUNCIATION: *roo-fuss hum-ing-bird*
RANGE: From southern Alaska to central Mexico
HABITAT: Parks, gardens, woodlands, meadows
FOOD: Nectar, insects
VOICE: *Chip chip chip,*
high-pitched *eeee*, squeaking

Rufous Hummingbirds are unusually tiny birds even when they're compared to other hummingbirds. They are a little less than 4 inches tall (9.5 cm) and weigh less than a nickel (3.4 g). Females have emerald green heads and backs, white throats and bellies, and rusty orange axillaries. Males have mostly rusty orange feathers from head to tail although some green feathers are present on their backs and heads. Males also have shiny orange throats and a small white patch directly underneath. The rusty orange color is commonly called *rufous*. Over 80 other birds of the world—like the Rufous Potoo and Rufous-bellied Chachalaca—are also named after their rufous-hued feathers.

Rufous Hummingbirds are famous for their extreme lifestyle. They will breed farther north than any other hummingbird species. Their breeding range can extend north of British Columbia and into lower parts of Alaska. These hummingbirds will spend April to July in their breeding range and then migrate south for the winter. Their migration route will take them down the west coast of Canada and the United States to central Mexico. They will spend their winters as far south as Oaxaca and return north in the spring. Rufous Hummingbirds can travel over 1,860 miles (3,000 km) during each migration!

Rufous Hummingbirds are well known for their antisocial behavior. These hummingbirds will fiercely protect their food and refuse to share space with other birds. The only time Rufous Hummingbirds care to be around other hummingbirds is during the mating season. Even then, males may chase females out of their territories.

BIZARRE BIRD FACT: Rufous Hummingbirds can beat their wings 52–62 times per second. This incredibly fast speed is what causes them to hum in flight and hover while feeding from flowers.

Scissor-tailed Flycatcher

•••••••

PRONUNCIATION: *si-zor tailed fly-catch-ur*
RANGE: From the south-central
United States to southern Mexico
HABITAT: Grasslands
FOOD: Insects
VOICE: *Pik-pik-pikpikpik*

Scissor-tailed Flycatchers are elegant birds with long scissor shaped tails. With their pale gray heads, white chests, gray backs, and black wings, Scissor-tailed Flycatchers may look pretty plain, but beneath their wings is a surprising splash of colorful feathers. Their reddish-orange axillaries, light pink sides, and pink undertail feathers are best seen when they zip and twirl through the air. Their amazingly long tails create an unmistakable silhouette against the sky.

You'll find Scissor-tailed Flycatchers in south-central U.S. states (Oklahoma, Kansas, Texas, Missouri, Arkansas, and Louisiana) during spring and summer. They're a common sight in rural and urban areas. Groups of adults and their fledglings can be spotted perched atop trees, along fence lines, and on utility poles near grassy fields. Look carefully for their nests in these areas as well. Before fall arrives, the flycatchers become more and more eager to migrate south to their wintering grounds in Mexico. They will begin to form large flocks with hundreds of flycatchers to migrate south together.

Watching Scissor-tailed Flycatchers perform acrobatic spins, dives, and flips to catch their prey is a highlight for many bird lovers. They will hunt alone for grasshoppers, beetles, and crickets. The birds are also known for their nearly constant chattering. Their voices sound like a squeaking dog toy being squeezed slowly at first then quickly.

BIZARRE BIRD FACT: Scissor-tailed Flycatchers have a habit of flying off-course from their migratory routes. These birds have been reported as far north as Alaska! That's almost 3,000 miles (4,828 km) away from their usual range.

Tree Swallow

• • ● • •

PRONUNCIATION: *swa-low*
RANGE: Throughout North America
HABITAT: Ocean and Arctic tundra
FOOD: Insects, seeds, berries
VOICE: Bubbly notes, twittering

Tree Swallows are small birds that are happy all over North America. In the summer, they are most commonly found throughout Alaska, Canada, and the northern half of the United States. In the fall, they will migrate through the southern half of the United States to spend their winter in Mexico. Female and male Tree Swallows can have similar appearances. Adults will have a white belly, a shiny blue-green head, and wings with black edges. Some females have fewer iridescent feathers and more grayish-brown feathers.

Despite their name, Tree Swallows surprisingly do not sit in trees outside of the nesting season. They are *cavity nesters*, which means they will build their homes inside of hollow tree branches. The rest of the year, Tree Swallows fly around open fields and lakes to chase insects in a series of acrobatic tumbles that showcase their greenish-blue iridescent feathers.

Compared to other swallows, Tree Swallows have unique diets since they can eat seeds and berries along with insects. During breeding months, they can be found eating old eggshells, clamshells, and fish bones for an added boost of calcium that will keep their own eggshells strong. If you live in their territory, you may find a Tree Swallow digging through your compost pile in search of the calcium-rich bits.

Tree Swallows are highly social, especially during the winter. At that time of year, they can be found migrating with thousands of their kind to Mexico. Around sunset, in a spectacular display of agility and teamwork, thousands of Tree Swallows will create a massive swirling vortex to funnel into their nighttime roosts among the reeds.

BIZARRE BIRD FACT: Tree Swallows drink water while flying. They will swoop down to the water surface and quickly skim their beak to get a sip.

Turkey Vulture

● ● ● ● ● ●

PRONUNCIATION: *tur-key vul-chur*
RANGE: From southern Canada to southern Mexico
HABITAT: Forests, open fields
FOOD: Carrion
VOICE: Usually silent, hissing

Turkey Vultures are large dark birds with huge wingspans and are fairly easy to identify without binoculars or cameras. In flight, Turkey Vultures are identified by their mostly dark brown bodies and the white bands of feathers on the underside of their wings. They fly with their 6-foot (2-m) wings slightly bent upward into a V shape, rarely beat their wings, and will gently rock left to right while soaring. When perched, their bright red, featherless heads and white bills are easier to see with the naked eye. The *turkey* in Turkey Vulture comes from their featherless heads that are wrinkly and red just like Wild Turkey heads. Black Vultures, the slightly smaller relatives of Turkey Vultures, look very similar but instead have black heads and white feathers only on the tips of their wings.

Turkey Vultures are famous for eating dead things off the street. In fact, they only eat dead things. As long as they are dead, mammals, birds, reptiles, fish, and bugs are all on the menu. They can smell a carcass from a mile away. And vultures are equipped with seriously strong stomachs—their stomach acid can kill viruses and dissolve bone. We owe many thanks to the scavengers that work as nature's cleaning crew.

In the Turkey Vulture's northern range, roadkill can freeze in cold winter weather and become impossible for them to eat. So Turkey Vultures migrate south and spend their winters in warmer regions of the continent where the carrion is kept at reasonable temperatures. During their migration it is typical to see large flocks of vultures flying in a circular formation. This cluster of birds is called a *kettle*. The kettle will swirl around on air currents that lift the soarers higher and higher into the sky.

BIZARRE BIRD FACT: Vultures are commonly called buzzards by many folks in North America. Buzzards are actually a type of hawk native to Europe not related to vultures.

Wild Turkey

• • • • • •

PRONUNCIATION: *tur-key*
RANGE: From southern Canada to central Mexico
HABITAT: Hardwood forests, open fields
FOOD: Seeds, nuts, insects, berries
VOICE: Gobbling, clucking

Wild Turkeys are very large birds with long legs and long, feather-less necks. They stand over 3 feet tall (1 m) and can weigh 20 pounds (9 kg). Both male and female turkeys have dark brown feathers with black barring all over and shiny metallic feathers on their bodies. The most unusual feature, however, is a flappy piece of skin called a *snood* that grows from the male's forehead and changes color and shape based on the turkey's mood. They also have bumps and wrinkles called *caruncles* on their faces that can change color. Male turkeys—known as toms—usually have bristly feathers called beards hanging from their chests and sharp spurs on the backs of their legs. They use these daggerlike growths to fight other males in the breeding season. Female turkeys—hens—can also have beards, but they do not have spurs.

Turkeys are famous for their loud gobbling and for display-ing their huge, fanned tails. Males put on a show for females by spreading all 16 of their fancy tail feathers. They puff up the rest of their body feathers to make themselves look extra big and gobble to get attention. When one male turkey gobbles, several others nearby will also begin gobbling.

If you've ever seen a turkey in the wild, it was probably not alone. After the breeding season, male turkeys hang out together in big groups separated from female turkeys. The females raise their chicks together in the summer then gather into groups with up to 200 females and young turkeys in the fall. Wild Turkeys can be found walking through forests and fields in large groups.

BIZARRE BIRD FACT: Wild Turkeys have some of the best vision in the animal kingdom. Everything in their view is always seen in focus.

Wood Thrush

• • ● • •

PRONUNCIATION: *wood thrush*
RANGE: Throughout eastern North America
HABITAT: Forests
FOOD: Insects, berries
VOICE: Musical, flutelike whistles

Wood Thrushes have reddish-brown heads, brown backs and wings, and white bellies with brown spots. They are migratory birds that spend their winters in southeastern Mexico then fly to the eastern United States to spend their summers. The Wood Thrush migration route requires the birds to fly across the Gulf of Mexico. The large body of water provides no stopping points, which means these birds must make it across in one long, continuous flight. In preparation for one of the most difficult journeys they will take, Wood Thrushes will chow down on high-energy berries to pack on fat reserves they can use during the nonstop flight. Wood Thrushes will also forage in leaf litter, searching for invertebrates to eat. They can be found hopping on the ground and scraping the forest floor with their long legs.

Have you heard the sound of a Wood Thrush? Their songs are very musical and delightful. The thrushes' tunes fill eastern woodlands in the summer. They are often the first birds to begin the dawn chorus and the last birds to sign off for the night. Wood Thrushes take the stage on leafless limbs of tall trees and sing airy, flutelike notes that instantly enchant the forest. The melodies cover the woodland with harmonies. Because of the unique anatomy of bird voice boxes, Wood Thrushes can sing multiple notes at the same time to produce melodic chords.

BIZARRE BIRD FACT: A large gathering of thrushes is called a *mutation*.

Yellow Warbler

• • • • • •

PRONUNCIATION: *war-blur*
RANGE: Throughout North America
HABITAT: Open woodlands
FOOD: Caterpillars, beetles, wasps, spiders
VOICE: High-pitched and musical
sweet-sweet-sweet-sweeter-than-sweet

The Yellow Warbler is a small bird in the warbler family. They can spend their summers anywhere between Alaska and southern Mexico but will migrate to Central and South America during the North American winter. Over 50 warbler species call North America home. Most of these warblers have some patches of yellow feathers somewhere on their bodies. As you can guess by their name, Yellow Warblers are the yellowest of all warblers. Female Yellow Warblers are pale yellow overall with grayish feathers on their wings. Males have bright yellow feathers all over with streaks of rusty red on their chests and black lines on their feathers.

The diet of the Yellow Warbler is made up mostly of caterpillars, beetles, wasps, and spiders. The warblers will hop around trees to pick bugs from the leaves and branches. This feeding style is called *gleaning*. You can find Yellow Warblers in a variety of places including woodlands, wetlands, and brushy thickets. They don't visit backyard bird feeders, but they are commonly spotted feeding or nesting in trees in urban areas.

Yellow Warblers sing an unmistakable song in the spring and summer. Their series of notes sounds as if the birds are singing *"sweet, sweet, sweet, sweeter-than-sweet."* They will repeat this song as often as 10 times in one minute. Yellow Warblers are very protective of their nests. When predators come too close, they use their alarm call to alert other birds in the area that danger is nearby. The Yellow Warblers will repeatedly call out *"seet seet seet"* and rush back to their nest to chase off any intruders.

BIZARRE BIRD FACT: Yellow Warblers that live in the eastern United States must fly over the Gulf of Mexico during migration in a single nonstop journey.

QUIZ

IF I WERE A BIRD...

Answer the questions below to determine
your bird personality!

1. Which school club would you most want to join?

A. Running Club

B. Swim Club

C. Art Club

D. Gardening Club

E. Science Club

2. What is your favorite recess activity?

A. A quick game of tag

B. Playing on the jungle gym

C. Chatting with friends

D. Doing cartwheels in the grass

E. Walking/roaming around the playground

3. How do you want to travel for your next vacation?

A. I'd rather stay at home.

B. Visit another part of the world.

C. Fly to the other side of the country.

D. Check out a fun city that is nearby.

E. Take a road trip across the state.

4. It's Wacky Hat Day at school. Which hat would you choose?

A. A cowboy hat

B. A big, floppy sun hat

C. A beanie

D. A baseball cap

E. No hat. I don't want to mess up my hair.

5. Your family has put you in charge of making dinner. What would be your favorite meal to make?

A. A big, juicy steak

B. A huge sushi plate

C. The biggest salad ever

D. A three-course meal

E. Pie. What's better than dessert for dinner?

ANSWERS

MOSTLY As: Greater Roadrunner—Greater Roadrunners are desert-dwelling birds that can handle the heat. They live year-round in some of the driest areas of North America. Roadrunners are very speedy birds that can run at 15 miles per hour (24 kph). Their speed and agility allow them to catch fast prey, like lizards, insects, and even birds. They spend most of their time alone but will also hang out with their mate. In their range, roadrunners are common neighborhood birds. They can be found sunbathing in gardens and searching the lawn for insects to eat.

MOSTLY Bs: Osprey—Ospreys are hawklike birds that live near large bodies of water. In the fall, Ospreys will migrate from the northern portions of North America to the southern United States, Mexico, and South America. During this migration, they will gather in groups for a short period. Ospreys mostly only eat fish, and they are very skilled at catching fish straight out of the water.

MOSTLY Cs: Dark-eyed Junco—Dark-eyed Juncos are a common bird found in North America. They become especially common in the

United States during the winter. Dark-eyed Juncos can look different depending on where they are from. It's as if each region has its own artistic color palette. There are six different junco color combinations. Which junco variety is found where you live? Dark-eyed Juncos are found along trails in the woods but also in suburban streets. Large groups of juncos will forage for seeds and insects.

MOSTLY Ds: Eastern Bluebird—Eastern Bluebirds are small birds found in open fields on farms and in parks. Bluebirds are one of the first birds that migrate to North America in the spring. They winter in Mexico and the southeastern United States and then fly as far north as Canada to spend the spring and summer. However, bluebirds in southern portions of North America will not migrate. There are plenty of bugs for them to call one place home all year long. During the breeding season, it's not uncommon to see a family of bluebirds sitting together on a fence. They flit off the fence to catch an insect and return to their perch.

MOSTLY Es: Turkey Vulture—Turkey Vultures are large birds with huge wingspans. They can soar for hours high up in the sky riding on air currents, hardly flapping their wings. They wander across the skies while searching for food. Turkey Vultures only eat dead things and can smell a carcass from a mile away. Their red heads are featherless so the vultures can eat without getting their feathers dirty. Turkey Vultures used to only be found in southern North America but now they can be found in Canada during spring and summer. Come winter, Turkey Vultures will migrate south and spend the coldest part of the year in warmer regions of the continent

Activities

Make Your Own Nature Journal

• • • • • •

This simple, creative exercise shows you how to make your very own nature journal to bring with you on your outings! You'll also find some prompts to get you started on how to use your journal.

NATURE JOURNAL MATERIALS

❖ 10 or more sheets of blank or lined paper

❖ 2 pieces of cardboard cut to match the size of paper

❖ Materials found in nature

❖ Stapler

❖ Glue

❖ Markers, crayons, colored pencils

DIRECTIONS

1. Place your paper between the two pieces of cardboard and staple them together along one edge.

2. Gather materials found in nature to use to decorate your nature journal. This includes objects like fallen leaves and twigs.

3. Glue your gathered materials to the cardboard covers and let them dry.

4. Color in any blank spaces with markers, crayons, and colored pencils.

5. Include this "Equipment Checklist" on the inside cover of your journal to make sure you have some of these essential items before your bird-watching outings:
   - Water and snacks
   - Comfortable clothes and shoes
   - Sunscreen
   - Binoculars
   - Field guide
   - Bug spray
   - Pen, pencil, colors

Journal Prompt 1—Bird Illustrations

Create a vision board of the different birds you'll see or hope to see on your outings. You can cut pictures of birds from magazines and paste them in to make a collage. Don't forget to leave room to sketch some of the birds you find, as well as plenty of space for recording notes on all the birds you spot while out and about!

Journal Prompt 2—Sit Spot

A *sit spot* is any place where you can sit and be still and enjoy nature. Spend five minutes sitting in your sit spot, and as you do, fill in the following information:

- The date
- The location of your sit spot
- The weather

Then, draw or write about the birds and plants you encounter during your time there.

At the end of your sit spot visit, write or draw how you feel being in nature during that moment.

Journal Prompt 3—Dig Deeper

Write your responses to the questions below and draw a picture that is inspired from your answers.

- What is your favorite season? Why?
- What is your favorite thing that lives outside? Why?
- If you could be a natural element—like an ocean, a cloud, lava, lightning, or a stone—which would you be? Why?
- When you go outside, which of your senses are you most thankful to have?

DIY Birdbath

• • ● • • •

Water is a vital but often overlooked resource we can provide birds to drink and bathe in. It's pretty easy to reuse something from around your house as a birdbath. Choose a small, shallow dish that is easy to clean and fill it with water. Things like a trash can lid, terracotta plate, old frying pan, or saucer are all good examples of items that could be used to hold water for birds. But if you really want to get creative, here is a cool birdbath you can make at home!

BIRDBATH MATERIALS

- 1–2 empty medium-size terracotta pots
- 1 old bowl, plate, or terracotta saucer
- Craft glue
- Tempura, acrylic, spray paint, or paint markers
- Paintbrushes
- Clear sealing paint
- A handful of medium-size rocks

DIRECTIONS

1. Clean any excess dirt from the containers you plan to use (bowl/plate/saucer and pots) and let them dry completely.

2. Flip one terracotta pot upside down and apply glue to the flat surface.

3. If you are using two pots, grab your second pot and sit it on top of the glue. The flat bottoms of both pots should be touching. Let the glue dry.

4. If you are using one pot, set the bowl/plate/saucer on the glue with the open side facing upward. The bowl/plate/saucer will be the water holder. If you are using two pots, add more glue to the rim of the second pot and set the bowl/plate/saucer on the glue with the open side facing upward. Let the glue dry.

5. Decorate the pots and bowls with paint. Allow the paint to dry.

6. Cover your decorated pots with the clear sealing paint. If you do not use sealing paint, your designs will fade over time. Apply this layer outdoors or in a well-ventilated area.

7. Place your birdbath outside where you want it to be—on a table or on the ground.

8. Gently place a few rocks on the bottom of the bowl. Birds can stand on the rocks to bathe and drink.

9. Add water to the bowl. Fill the bowl to a level so that the water is a little below the rocks. Birds don't need very deep water. They prefer shallow puddles.

10. Wait for the birds to find it, and refill the water as needed.

DIY Bird Feeder

······

Setting up a bird feeder is a good way to provide year-round nutrition for birds. (**TIP:** Do your best to keep the food dry at all times. Wet seeds can grow harmful bacteria and fungi. It's best to pick up and throw away any food that gets wet.) Birds will really enjoy visiting your yard if you have a feeder with their favorite seeds. (Squirrels will also enjoy the free snacks!) Try making this feeder to help out your neighborhood birds—and to reuse one thing to keep it from going to the landfill.

BIRD FEEDER MATERIALS

❖ A gallon milk jug, 2-liter soda bottle, or other large drink container and its lid

❖ Scissors

❖ 2 twigs or long wooden sticks

❖ Acrylic paint

❖ Paintbrushes

❖ 24 inches of string or yarn

❖ Bird seed mix (any mix that includes whole black oil sunflower seeds)

DIRECTIONS

1. Wash and dry the lid and empty container.

2. Cut a small X on all four sides of the container, near the bottom.

3. Slide the twigs or sticks through the Xs. At least 1 inch of twig should stick out from the sides of the container. The birds will use these as perches.

4. Cut a horizontal rectangle above each perch. The birds will reach the seeds through these holes.

5. Decorate the container with paint.

6. Poke a hole through the cap and thread the string through.

7. Add seeds to the container. (**TIP:** Put the seeds in from the top rather than the sides.)

8. Screw on the cap and hang the feeder from a tree or pole.

TIP: In the spring and summer, birds may not visit your feeder as often. The warmer seasons provide a bunch of bugs and berries for the birds to forage. You can expect many more visitors in the fall and winter when plants and insects are dormant because of the cold weather.

DIY Window Decals

• • ❂ • • •

Window collisions are a major threat to birds. You can help prevent them by adding anti–window collision stickers and decals to your windows. Try these DIY window decals as seasonal decorations that also help save birds' lives.

WINDOW DECAL MATERIALS

+ Printed or drawn stencils to trace
+ Piece of paper and pen or pencil
+ 2 tablespoons washable craft glue
+ ¼ teaspoon dish soap
+ A small bowl
+ A plate (optional)
+ Food coloring (optional)
+ Cookie cutter
+ A sandwich bag or plastic wrap
+ Tape or a paperweight
+ Paintbrush
+ Permanent markers for decorating

DIRECTIONS

1. Draw or print your stencil design on a piece of paper.

2. Mix the glue and soap together in a small bowl.

3. If you would like to make multiple colors, pour the glue mixture onto a plate and mix in food coloring, as needed.

4. Place the cookie cutter on top of the sandwich bag/sheet. Or place your stencil underneath the plastic wrap.

5. Secure the plastic wrap to the table with tape or a paperweight.

6. Use the paintbrush to paint an even layer of the glue mixture onto the stencil. You may need to paint multiple coats.

7. Let the decals sit out and dry. (This will take several hours.)

8. After the decals have dried completely, you can decorate them further with permanent markers.

9. After the ink dries, peel the decals from the plastic.

10. Spray the side that you didn't color with a light mist of water and stick that side against the outside of the window.

TIP: If your decals start falling off, simply spray the back of the decal with a light mist of water.

SELECTED ADDITIONAL RESOURCES

FIELD GUIDE BOOKS

Check your library for more resources:

Golden Field Guide—Birds of North America

Kaufman Guide to Birds of North America

National Geographic Kids Bird Guide of North America

Peterson Field Guide to Birds of North America

The Sibley Guide to Birds

ONLINE FIELD GUIDES

All About Birds—https://www.allaboutbirds.org

Audubon Guide to North American Birds—
  https://www.audubon.org/bird-guide

Birds of the World—https://www.birdsoftheworld.org

Xeno-Canto—https://xeno-canto.org

WATCH BIRDS VIRTUALLY AT HOME

https://www.mangolinkcam.com/webcams/birds/feeders
  -north-america.html

https://birdcams.live

https://www.audubon.org/birdcams

https://www.allaboutbirds.org/cams/